The
Tarantula

An Owner's Guide To

A HAPPY HEALTHY PET

Howell Book House

DISCARDED

Howell Book House
A Simon & Schuster Macmillan Company
1633 Broadway
New York, NY 10019

Macmillan Publishing books may be purchased for business or sales promotional use. For information please write: Special Markets Department, Macmillan Publishing USA, 1633 Broadway, New York, NY 10019.

Library of Congress Cataloging-in-Publication Data

Flank, Lenny, Jr.
The tarantula / by Lenny Flank, Jr.
p. cm.—(An owner's guide to a happy healthy pet)
ISBN 0-87605-601-X
1. Tarantulas as pets.   I. Howell Book House   II. Series
SF459.T37T37   1998
639'.7—dc21   98-14485
                       CIP

Manufactured in the United States of America
10 9 8 7 6 5 4 3 2 1

Series Director: Amanda Pisani
Series Assistant Director: Rich Thomas
Book Design: Michele Laseau
Cover Design: Iris Jeromnimon
Illustration: Laura Robbins
Photography:
  Front cover photo by Sherry Lee Harris; inset photo by Sam Marshall;
    back cover photo by Sam Marshall
Joan Balzarini: 6, 88, 99
Lenny Flank, Jr.: 9, 60, 63, 64, 68, 72, 73, 80, 82, 103
Sherry Lee Harris: 34, 36–37, 42, 96, 97, 113, 114, 116
Bill Love: 12, 13, 17, 22, 39, 45, 49, 51, 78, 86–87, 92
Sam Marshall: Title page, 11, 18, 26, 27, 40, 43, 44, 46, 47, 48, 50, 52, 53, 54, 55, 77, 95, 98, 102, 106, 118, 121, 122
David Schilling: 2–3, 5, 20, 38, 62, 70, 85, 90, 91, 110
Production Team: Chris Van Camp, Clint Lahnen, Angel Perez, Dennis Sheehan, Terri Sheehan

Contents

Welcome
to the
World

of the
Tarantula

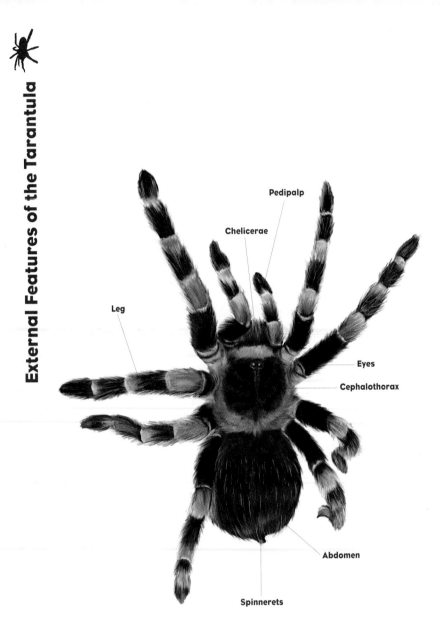

External Features of the Tarantula

Pedipalp

Chelicerae

Leg

Eyes

Cephalothorax

Abdomen

Spinnerets

What Is a Tarantula?

When most people see a spider scurrying across the floor, their first instinct is to mash it flat with the nearest shoe or rolled-up magazine. The suggestion that spiders, and particularly such large and "horrid-looking" spiders as tarantulas, would make interesting and attractive pets would be met with blank 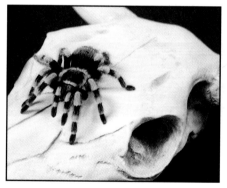 stares, or perhaps a gentle suggestion that a visit to the shrink might be in order.

Despite this widespread revulsion toward spiders, however, the number of people who keep these animals as pets is growing steadily. Until recently, the number of tarantula species widely available for collectors could be counted on the fingers of one hand; today, several commercial dealers make their living by selling (and sometimes breeding) tarantula species from around the world. Each year, more and more people who are looking for an unusual pet that doesn't take up much space, is inexpensive to maintain and doesn't require a lot of elaborate equipment, are turning to tarantulas.

Is a Tarantula Right for You?

Here are some things to consider before you purchase

your spider: Tarantulas are long-lived animals. Life spans of ten years or longer are common, and the females of some species will live up to thirty years. Purchasing a spider like this can be a decades-long commitment.

With very few exceptions, tarantulas are for looking, not touching. Keeping a tarantula in a terrarium is more like maintaining a tropical fish tank than it is like keeping a hamster or turtle.

If you are looking to receive affection or cuddling from your pet, then a tarantula is not for you. Spiders are absolutely incapable

Your first step should be to decide if a tarantula is the right pet for you.

of developing any emotional attachment to their keepers. They will never grow to "love" you, and, like all wild animals, if they feel threatened in any way they will act to defend themselves.

Above all, if your reason for keeping a tarantula is to show off and impress your friends with how macho you are, tarantulas are definitely not for you. Go take karate lessons instead.

Evolutionary History

The early history of spiders is very poorly known, because, unlike dinosaurs and other vertebrates, arachnids lack skeletons or hard body parts that can be easily fossilized. On rare occasions, spiders are preserved in fossilized tree sap, known as amber. Even more seldom, the soft bodies may be preserved as imprints in fine-grained limestone or sandstone. Some information about the evolutionary history of spiders can also be revealed by careful anatomical comparison between various living groups of arthropods. All of this information allows us to piece together a rough picture of the evolutionary history of the arachnids.

The arthropods, the group to which spiders and tarantulas belong, are evolutionary descendants of the very ancient segmented worms known as the *Annelida*. These animals were constructed in a series of rings or segments, each externally identical to those before and after it, with a mouth at one end and an anal opening at the other. Each segment contained a number of sensory bristles or hairs. The annelids are one of the earliest of the multicellular organisms, and fossil traces of these animals date all the way back to pre-Cambrian times, over one-half billion years ago. The earliest segmented worms lived with such other ancient animals as jellyfish and sponges. Modern annelids include the common earthworm or nightcrawler, known by the scientific name *Lumbricus terrestris*.

Through the process of evolution, most biologists conclude, one group of annelids underwent a process of modification, which resulted in the birth of the arthropods. Each body segment developed a pair of walking legs. The first six segments of the annelid ancestor were fused together to produce a head, which contained a number of simple eyes. The appendages in these fused segments were modified to form mouthparts and, later, some of these were transformed into chelicerae and pedipalps.

Finally, crude structures for gas exchange and respiration, called booklungs, allowed the new arthropods to emerge from the sea and become the first animals to live on land.

Although the arthropods were one of the oldest groups of terrestrial animals, they appeared originally as marine creatures. One of the most important arthropod groups in the fossil record are the eurypterids, or "water scorpions," which are found in deposits from the Silurian period some 450 million years ago. In the process of evolving from their proto-arthropod ancestors, these creatures had fused nearly all of their body segments into two distinct body sections—the abdomen and cephalothorax—as well as modifying a number of the foremost appendages into mouthparts, chelicerae and pedipalps. These aquatic animals resembled the modern-day scorpions. Most were tiny, but a few, including such widespread genera as *Carcinosoma* and *Pterygotus*, reached lengths of over 3 feet and were fearsome predators, seizing other marine animals with their large claws. It is believed that the eurypterids, or a group closely related to them, are the ancestors of all the terrestrial arachnids.

TRIGS

One of the earliest known groups of terrestrial arachnids are the trigonotarbids (referred to by arachnologists the world over as "trigs"). Fossil remains of these animals date back to the upper Silurian period, around 420 million years ago. The trigs appear to have evolved from one of the advanced aquatic eurypterid groups by replacing the aquatic gills of their ancestor with primitive booklungs for breathing air. (The terrestrial scorpions, which also appear in the fossil record at about this time, were descended from another branch of the eurypterids and underwent a similar process of becoming air-breathers.)

The trigs were small animals, some ⅛ inch in length, with eight walking legs, two pedipalplike organs and four booklungs.

They also had a distinct cephalothorax and abdomen, though the abdomen was still segmented. Unlike later spiders, the trigs lacked fangs and had no spinnerets (the presence of spinnerets is generally held to be the distinguishing characteristic of a fossil spider).

One group within the trigs, known as the palaeocharinids, were particularly spiderlike in their construction. Several well-preserved examples of this family, known as *Palaeocharinus,* have been found in England, and date back to almost 400 million years ago. Unlike the other trigs, which had a single pair of eyes in the middle front of the cephalothorax, *Palaeocharinus* also had lateral eyes with multiple lenses, which, some arachnologists have concluded, may have given rise to the two large central eyes and several smaller lateral eyes found in modern spiders.

One group of palaeocharinids appears to have diverged to form a widespread group of trigs known as the anthracomartids, which were the most common arachnids of their time. Today, most authorities postulate that another group of palaeocharinids are the probable ancestors of the modern spiders. When the anthracomartids finally died out, just before the dinosaurs appeared, the spiders were waiting in the wings to take over and invade these ecological niches.

The eurypterids were ancient ancestors of modern spiders and scorpions. This 420 million-year-old fossil was found in New York.

The earliest recognizable spider that has been preserved in the fossil record has been given the Latin name *Attercopus fimbriunguis.* It was found in the state of New York and dates to about 380 million years ago. An older fossil, named *Palaeocteniza crassipes,* is very spiderlike but lacks spinnerets. It is uncertain whether *Palaeocteniza crassipes* is a direct ancestor of the spiders.

Based on behavioral characteristics of existing spiders, as well as the structure of the few fossil traces that have been found, it is speculated that the earliest terrestrial spiders were burrowing animals.

Over time, some groups of spiders left their burrows and took up a more open existence. Some took to climbing low plants and shrubs and spinning elaborate orb webs to capture flying prey. Others took to running on the ground to actively pursue their prey. And a few groups stuck to the sedentary burrowing existence of their ancestors. Thus, most arachnologists believe that the group to which the tarantulas belong, the mygalomorphs, are very similar in their structure and habits to the earliest primitive land spiders.

One of the earliest known fossil mygalomorphs was found in Argentina and has been dated at around 300 million years. Named *Megarachne*, it has a body length of 3 inches and an estimated leg span of almost 20 inches. Another fossil mygalomorph was found in France, and dates to about 240 million years ago, during the Triassic period—the time when the dinosaurs were first rising to prominence. This fossil spider is scarcely distinguishable from its modern relatives. It is likely that the mygalomorphs evolved even earlier than these, but have not yet been discovered in these earlier deposits. The tarantulas belong to a family within the mygalomorphs known as the theraphosids.

Many of the arboreal species of tarantula are found in habitats that have cyclical wet and dry seasons and are thus prone to periodic flooding (the Indian ornamental and the Latin American pinktoes are good examples). Speculatively, these groups began as burrowing spiders, but took up an arboreal lifestyle as a way of avoiding flooded burrows. If this is true, then the arboreal species may be the most recent and most specialized group of living tarantulas.

Ecology

As the earth revolves around the sun, certain areas of the globe are better positioned to capture sunlight and thus are more energy-rich than other areas. Because energy is unevenly distributed over the earth's surface, the biosphere is divided into several distinct climate zones. In turn, these climate zones support a characteristic set of plant and animal life, which interact with each other to form a unique ecosystem.

Within each of these ecosystems, particular organisms play specific roles, according to the habitat they require, the food they eat and other environmental needs. This interlocking set of requirements is called the animal's niche. In the tropical rain forest ecosystem, for example, one niche may consist of a ground-dwelling spider that lies in ambush at the entrance to its burrow and feeds on passing insects and small vertebrates. Another spider's niche may be an arboreal existence in the low canopy, hunting for insects and small vertebrates.

The typical habitat in the equatorial regions is the tropical forest ecosystem, which takes advantage of the high energy input provided by the sun as well as an abundance of water to produce an amazing diversity of life. Tropical rain forests are the most prolific ecosystems on the planet and may contain as many as half of all living species.

The climate of the tropical forest is hot and humid. Temperatures run into the 90s (°F) during the day, dropping to the high 70s at night. In addition, it showers almost every day in the tropics, producing ambient humidity as high as 90 percent. The warm and humid conditions of the rain forest are ideal for tarantulas, allowing them to maintain the preferred body temperature year-round, as well as to find the high humidity levels they need. Most living tarantulas are tropical in range, and a large proportion of the pet tarantulas you are likely to encounter will be native to tropical rain forests in Latin America, Asia or Africa. The dense canopy and periodic rainy seasons, along with the abundance of food, make an arboreal lifestyle particularly inviting, and nearly all of the arboreal tarantulas can be found in rain forest habitats.

The hot, humid climate of the rain forest provides a perfect home for many species of tarantula.

The desert ecosystem is marked by very hot, dry conditions with little or no moisture. About one-third of the earth's surface is covered by desert, including the large Sahara region of Africa, the Gobi Desert in Asia and the several deserts making up the southwestern United States and northern Mexico. Rainfall in these areas is sporadic at best, and plants and animals must engage in a constant struggle to avoid the lethal heat and lack of moisture. Desert animals must also be able to combat cold, for temperatures drop sharply at night. Food sources are rare, and species diversity is usually very low. Most desert species avoid the heat of the day and the cold of the night by staying in underground burrows or by burying themselves in the sand, emerging when temperatures are suitable. They get most of the water they need from their food.

A number of tarantulas, and many of those found in the United States, are desert-dwellers. Their low need for food allows them to live in this spartan environment. Desert tarantulas spend the hot daylight hours in the deep recesses of their burrows, emerging at dusk to wait in ambush for a passing prey animal.

Spiders

*Spiders range
from tiny . . .*

Spiders are one of the most numerous and diverse groups of organisms on earth. There are some 36,000 known species of spider, and most arachnologists suspect that there may be at least that many more that have not yet been scientifically described. By comparison, there are around 4,600 known species of mammals and about 2,700 species of snakes. In size, spiders range from the Goliath birdeating tarantula *Theraphosa blondi* of Latin America, with a body more than 4 inches long and a leg span of over 10 inches, to the tiny *Patu marplesi* spider of the Samoan islands, which is about the size of the period at the end of this sentence.

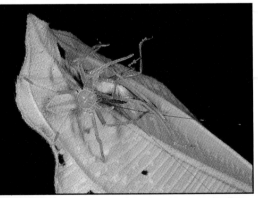

Spiders are found on virtually every landmass, and have even been observed floating on silken "balloons" over 200 miles out at sea. They have invaded almost every conceivable niche, including deserts, tropical rain forests, prairies and deciduous woods. The North American fishing spiders live along the shores of ponds and lakes and are capable of walking across the surface of the water to capture insects, tadpoles and small fish. There is even a species of fully aquatic spider, which survives underwater by carrying a bubble of air along with it. Several other spiders live in extremely close contact with humans, inhabiting woodpiles, cellars and the spaces under floors and between walls. No matter where you are right now, the chances are very good that there is a spider living somewhere within 10 feet of you.

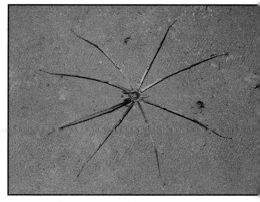

ARTHROPODS

Spiders are members of the phylum of living organisms known as the *Arthropoda*. Arthropods (the name comes from the Greek words for "joint foot") are characterized by a hard external skeleton and a number of jointed legs. Perhaps as many as 85 percent of all living animal species are arthropods. The arthropod group includes all of the insects, which, by themselves, are the largest group of living organisms. Although many uninformed people refer to spiders as "bugs," in reality there are several obvious differences between spiders and insects. For example, spiders have eight walking legs while insects have only six, and spiders have two divisions in their body while insects have three.

The various marine crabs and lobsters are crustaceans, which are also arthropods and are related to the terrestrial insects and spiders. The centipedes and millipedes are also members of the arthropod group.

13

Spiders and scorpions are included in the class of arthropods known as arachnids. Spiders in particular are classified in the order *Araneae*. As a group, spiders can be identified by their unique body structure, which consists of a two-part body—a cephalothorax (containing a fused head and thorax), and an abdomen with spinnerets. Spiders also have eight jointed walking legs and a smaller pair of sensory appendages called pedipalps. Tarantulas, like most spiders, have eight eyes. (The number of eyes in other families of spiders varies from as many as twelve to as few as two.)

FAMILIES OF SPIDERS

Among the most familiar of the spider families are the *Salticidae,* or jumping spiders, and the various species of orbweavers, which are found in the family *Araneidae*. The familiar brown cellar spider is a member of the *Pholcidae* family. Two North American spiders that are noted for the potency of their venom are the widows (*Latrodactus* species), which belong to the family *Theridiidae,* and the brown recluse (*Loxosceles reclusa*), which is classified in the family *Sicariidae*. Neither of these are closely related to the tarantulas. The wolf spiders of the family *Lycosidae* are terrestrial hunters who do not spin webs, but pursue their prey on the ground. The wolf spiders and the tarantulas look vaguely alike, but again, they are not very closely related.

MYGALOMORPHS

The tarantulas belong to an infraorder of spiders called *Mygalomorphae* (sometimes also referred to in older books as *Orthognathae*). The mygalomorphs are distinguished from other spiders by anatomical differences in the spinnerets and other organs. As a group, the mygalomorphs are very primitive and still retain many of the characteristics of the earliest spiders.

Within the mygalomorph infraorder are a number of other families and subgroups. One of these families, the *Ctenizidae,* contains the trapdoor spiders and another, the *Hexathelidae*, contains the Australian funnelweb spiders. The purseweb spiders belong to the family *Atypidae*. All of these spiders closely resemble tarantulas but are distinguished by a relative lack of body hair, a differing structure of their feet and claws and other anatomical details.

WHAT'S IN A NAME?

The tarantulas are grouped in the family *Theraphosidae*. Although the general public usually refers to any large hairy spider as a "tarantula," to an arachnologist, and for the purposes of this book, the name "tarantula" refers specifically to the 800 or so members of the theraphosid family of spiders.

BODY TEMPERATURE

Spiders are ectothermic, or cold-blooded, and therefore are dependent upon outside sources of heat to maintain their body temperatures. Ectothermic animals cannot produce enough body heat metabolically to maintain their body temperatures at the desired level, and instead take on the same temperature as their surroundings, which may explain why most large spiders are found in warm areas such as rain forests and deserts. Heat can be thought of as the spider's "fuel"—the warmer they are, the more rapid their biochemical processes become and the better they are able to perform tasks such as feeding and reproducing.

An important advantage of an ectothermic metabolism is its low need for energy input. Because ectothermic animals use outside sources of energy to maintain their body temperature, they do not need to devote food resources to this end, and can therefore survive on a much lower amount of food energy—most tarantulas can do quite well on one meal every week, and all are capable of going for months without food if necessary.

VENOM AND FANGS

One of the questions most frequently asked by beginners is, "Are tarantulas poisonous?" Tarantulas, like nearly all spiders, are venomous; that is, they possess toxins inside their bodies and they have fangs for introducing this venom into other organisms. Whether that venom is medically significant to humans, however, is another question entirely.

The venom apparatus is used to procure food by paralyzing prey animals for the spider to feed on, but the fangs can also be used as defensive weapons if the need arises.

For nearly all tarantulas, despite their forbidding appearance and their sometimes frightening and threatening display, a bite is no more serious than a hornet sting. There are no confirmed instances of a human death caused by the direct effects of tarantula venom, and tarantulas are not considered a significant medical problem anywhere.

The tarantula's fangs are kept folded under the front of the cephalothorax, out of view. When the fangs of a large theraphosid are opened in a threat posture, it's an impressive sight. The fangs of some of the larger tarantulas are capable of penetrating through a human fingernail. The tip of each fang has a small opening, through which venom is forced out from the glands.

The chelicerae and fangs of a tarantula are unusual in that they open and close from front to back, like a pair of pocket knives; in most other spiders, the chelicerae and fangs open and close from side to side, like a pair of scissors. In most other spiders, the venom glands also extend back from the chelicerae into the front of the cephalothorax.

During feeding, the sharp fangs are used to penetrate the tough chitinous cuticle of an insect, and muscular contractions in the chelicerae force venom into the prey's body. The venom works by killing or paralyzing the prey. The venom apparatus of the tarantula originally evolved as a method of obtaining food, and its defensive role is probably secondary.

The amount of venom injected appears to be under the muscular control of the spider, and in some instances, when a tarantula bites in self-defense, it may not release any venom at all—a phenomenon known as a "dry bite."

EXOSKELETON

Spiders are invertebrates and do not have any internal skeletal system. They also differ significantly from more traditional pets in such basic matters as circulation, respiration and locomotion.

Because spiders lack an internal skeletal structure and have no bones, they have a hard cuticle or exoskeleton made mostly of the protein chitin, which is somewhat like plastic in its physical properties. Chitin provides the two essentials needed by any terrestrial creature— it is nearly waterproof and prevents the animal from desiccating, and it provides a support structure that allows the animal's organs and internal systems to resist the stress of gravity.

Scorpions, like tarantulas and other arachnids, have exoskeletons.

The arthropod cuticle is constructed in several layers. The inner layer is made up of the epidermis. The cells of the epidermis are alive and secrete the chitin that makes up the outer shell. The middle layer of the exoskeleton is made up of soft, flexible chitin that provides elasticity, allowing the spider to absorb impacts. The outer layer is also made of chitin, but it has been stiffened and hardened by the addition of other materials and forms a hard protective exterior. In areas

17

where flexibility is necessary, such as the limb joints and the abdomen (which must be able to expand and contract during feeding), the rigid outer layer is missing or is much thinner.

A series of muscles are attached to the inside of the spider's external skeleton. These muscles are attached in such a manner that they can curl the limbs and pull them inward, but cannot pull them outward. To straighten its appendages, a spider must force blood into them, using hydraulic pressure to push them into a straightened position. For this reason, a spider that is dehydrated cannot produce the necessary blood pressure, and therefore it cannot straighten its legs properly.

Molting

The exoskeleton is comprised of dead cells and thus cannot expand. As the tarantula grows, the cuticle becomes tighter and tighter. Periodically, it must be shed or molted to allow the spider to continue growing.

A tarantula molts throughout its lifetime so it can continue growing.

The tarantula is very vulnerable during the molting process, and thus it usually retreats to a safe spot to carry out this procedure. Young and growing spiderlings may shed every few weeks, while adults shed only once per year and may even skip years.

CEPHALOTHORAX

The cephalothorax is composed of the fused head and thorax, which in arachnids appears to form one continuous body section. The cephalothorax is joined to the abdomen by a narrow waist called the pedicel. With the exception of the spinnerets, all of the spider's appendages, including the legs, pedipalps and chelicerae, are connected to the cephalothorax.

The top of the cephalothorax is protected by a hard plate called the carapace. The little dimple in the top of a tarantula's carapace is known as the fovea and is the spot where the stomach muscles attach to the spider's exoskeleton (the muscles attach to a little cone on the internal surface of the carapace known as an apodeme).

ABDOMEN

The abdomen is the large bulbous section at the rear of the tarantula's body. It contains most of the spider's vital organs. The long tubelike heart runs along the top of the abdomen, and beneath the heart lie the intestines with their numerous branching caeca. The reproductive organs, the booklungs and the silk glands take up much of the rest of the abdominal cavity.

Externally, the abdomen is covered with hairs. The long fingerlike spinnerets are the only appendages attached to the abdomen, and these are found at the rear, just above the external anal opening.

On the underside of the abdomen, you will see the genital opening near the pedicel and, on either side of this, the two openings to the booklungs.

HAIRS

The exterior of a tarantula's body is covered with long bristlelike hairs, known as setae. Some of the various types of hair contain a sensory cell and a nerve ending in their hollow base. When such a hair is stimulated, it triggers a response in the sensory cell. Individual hairs may be sensitive to motion, heat, cold and other environmental triggers. Hairs near the mouth and chelicerae are capable of sensing chemicals, which gives the spider a rudimentary sense of taste and smell.

It seems clear that most species, being nocturnal burrowers, obtain much of the information they have about their surroundings through their sensory hairs. These are extraordinarily responsive; terrestrial tarantulas are extremely sensitive to vibrations transmitted through the ground and can detect a footfall at a considerable distance. Theraphosids have no ears and are therefore incapable of detecting airborne sounds (although they can pick up vibrations through the substrate or with silken triplines).

Urticating Hairs

The hairs on the abdomen of most North and South American tarantulas have been further modified to serve as defensive weapons. These "urticating hairs" possess sharp tips with microscopic barbs. When threatened, the spider will use its back legs to kick off a cloud of urticating hairs at its attacker. In some species, such as the *Avicularia,* the urticating hairs must be physically pushed into the target. The sharp barbed points burrow into the skin like tiny porcupine quills, producing an itchy rash that can be very irritating. Spiders that have repeatedly cast off their urticating hairs develop large bald spots on their abdomen, with the pinkish-colored cuticle layer exposed. The urticating hairs are replaced the next time the spider molts.

A large bald spot is usually the result of a spider having released its urticating hairs.

The African and Asian tarantulas are not known to have urticating hairs. Most arboreal species also seem to lack them. However, many old-world species (along with a number of new-world species) possess a set of modified hairs that serve another purpose. These species have stiff hairs on their legs, pedipalps or chelicerae that can be rapidly rubbed together to produce an audible hissing sound, which the spider uses as a threat display—a phenomenon known as stridulating.

Eyes

Tarantulas possess eight eyes that are clumped together at the front of the carapace. Each eye consists of a bundle of light-sensitive cells that are covered by a single lens, formed from a clear thickening in the outer cuticle. Each light-sensitive cell in the retina has a nerve fiber that gathers into a nerve that feeds directly into the ganglia in the spider's nervous system. Scientists have found indications that at least some of the arboreal theraphosids may have relatively good vision. Nevertheless, the terrestrial burrowers, at least, do not seem to depend very much on visual information; they seem to rely mostly on their sensory hairs.

Legs

Like all spiders, tarantulas have eight walking legs, arranged in four pairs and all attached to the bottom of the cephalothorax. Each leg contains seven sections, separated from each other by flexible joints. Muscles between the joints allow the spider to bend its legs inwards, while blood pressure is utilized to push the joints open and extend the legs.

Each leg has an internal seal between the coxa and trochanter, which closes off to prevent blood loss if the leg is torn off or lost. The spider is capable of voluntarily dropping off its leg if it is injured, and will then seal the remaining joint surfaces to prevent blood loss (this mechanism is known as autotomy). The spider will then sometimes eat the detached leg to recover the proteins and nutrients it contains.

Feet

Each foot contains two small claws. The feet are also padded by tufts of hair, called scopulae, that provide traction. The feet of arboreal spiders are usually noticeably wider and longer than those of terrestrials.

PEDIPALPS

A tarantula's pedipalps (sometimes referred to simply as "palps") look like walking legs, but are shorter (they contain only six sections instead of the seven found in the walking legs). They are located at the front of

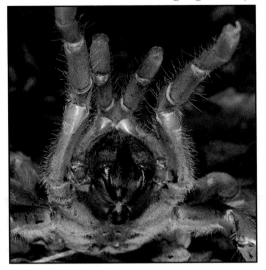

the tarantula's body, next to the chelicerae and just in front of the first pair of walking legs. The palps are evolved from a pair of appendages on the ancestral arthropod. Tarantulas depend heavily on their sense of touch to provide them with information about their surroundings. The pedipalps are heavily loaded with sensory hairs, and the spider uses them to feel its

This tarantula is not happy (notice the fangs and palps).

way as it walks along. The palps can also be used to manipulate prey while it is being eaten. When most tarantulas feel threatened, they rear up on their back legs and raise the palps high in the air, exposing the opened fangs.

SPINNERETS

Like all spiders, tarantulas produce silk. The tarantula's spinnerets are located at the very end of the abdomen; they look like long fingerlike projections with numerous joints. Most spiders have four or six spinnerets—the more primitive tarantulas have two large spinnerets and two much smaller ones. The spinnerets are controlled by a complex set of muscles and are capable of intricate and delicate motions.

HEART AND BLOOD

Spider blood is a liquid that is usually pale blue. The tarantula's heart consists of a hollow tube that runs almost the length of the abdomen. The squeezing action of the heart forces blood to circulate from one end of the body through the aorta to the other, carrying nutritional substances and oxygen with it. The blood then seeps back into the heart through a series of inlet holes along the sides, to be pumped out again. Tarantulas have an "open" circulatory system; the blood is not confined to vessels but fills the body cavity and bathes all of the internal organs.

LUNGS

The respiratory system of tarantulas is very primitive, even for a spider. Tarantulas do not possess any tracheal tubes. Instead, they have a structure formed from a cavity within the abdominal wall. Inside this chamber, the cuticle is very thin and is folded into a series of pleats, called lamellae. Because these pleated structures somewhat resemble the pages of a book, this type of breathing apparatus is known as a booklung. Air diffuses into this chamber through a slit on the underside of the abdomen and passes between the pleated folds in the booklung, where gas is exchanged through the thin cuticle. Oxygen is then picked up by the blood and is distributed to the other body tissues.

GENITALS

The genital opening in tarantulas is located on the underside of the abdomen, near the pedicel. In males, this opening leads to the testes, which produce sperm. In females, the genital opening is located within a fold called the epigastric furrow, and it leads to the ovaries where eggs are produced. When the female reaches sexual maturity, she develops two tiny pouches inside the epigastric furrow called "spermathacae," where live sperm can be stored after breeding. These pouches are shed along with the rest of the cuticle whenever the spider molts. Shed skins can be closely examined to determine whether the female is in reproductive condition or not. Only mature females will have well-developed spermathacae.

Because female spiders are capable of storing live sperm inside the spermathecae, they can thus produce viable eggs for some time after a mating. But because these storage sacks are shed along with the rest of the skin, a female that has recently molted will not be able to lay fertile eggs until she mates again.

In captivity, females in good condition continuously produce eggs inside of their bodies. Usually, these unfertilized eggs will be resorbed by the body. In some cases, however, the eggs will be laid as if they were fertile, and captive female spiders that have not mated will therefore sometimes produce an eggsac. These eggs are not fertilized and they will not hatch. The female may guard them faithfully for a while, only to give up and eat them to recycle their nutrients.

STOMACH

Because tarantulas cannot ingest solid food, their digestive system is designed to deal with liquid food only. The spider's venom acts by interfering with the nervous system of the prey (neurotoxic venom) or by breaking down the body tissues (cytotoxic venom). To digest its prey, the tarantula vomits a mixture of digestive enzymes onto its food, breaking the tissues down into a liquid that can then be sucked up through the spider's mouthparts into an enlarged section of the digestive tube known as the "sucking stomach." Powerful muscles in the cephalothorax pull on the stomach and expand it to create the sucking action.

Once the liquid food is drawn into the digestive tube, it is broken down by enzymes until it is reduced to molecules small enough to pass directly through the walls of the gut and into the bloodstream. These nutritive chemicals are then carried to all of the body tissues. Waste products are collected and carried by the Malphigian tubes to the anus, at the rear of the abdomen, where they are expelled. Spider droppings consist mostly of uric acid crystals and are usually dry and chalklike.

BRAIN

The nervous system of a tarantula is extremely primitive. A large nerve cord runs along the spider's cephalothorax, underneath the carapace. Although a large mass of nerve tissue near the eyes is referred to as the spider's "brain," it shares most of its function with another nerve mass along the central cord, and these are referred to collectively as the ganglia. Nerve fibers from the sensory hairs run to the ganglia and provide the tarantula with most of its information. Nerves also run from the ganglia to the muscles, eyes and other organs.

Tarantulas neither possess nor have need for any great intelligence. Much of their behavior is inborn and controlled by the spider's genes. For the most part, they seem to respond instinctively to whatever external stimuli they encounter. Their two basic rules in life seem to be (1) "If it moves and is smaller than me, I'll eat it" and (2) "If it moves and is larger than me, I'll bite it or run away from it."

Tarantulas do, however, possess an ability to retain memories and are capable of learning. Captive spiders will sometimes reject prey animals that apparently smell or taste bad, such as certain beetles and cockroaches. After such an incident, they will subsequently refuse to attack that particular prey animal, demonstrating that they have at least a rudimentary ability to learn from experience.

They also demonstrate a certain amount of curiosity. If a new object is placed in its cage, the tarantula will often wander over and investigate it, tapping it with its palps. So, although your tarantula will never learn to sit up or fetch your slippers, it is not completely mindless.

Hunting and Webs

Tarantulas do not capture their prey with webs. Instead, most are ambush hunters who lie in wait for a likely meal to pass by before leaping upon it and overpowering it with their fangs. Some of the arboreal species are active hunters that run down their prey and capture it, and some terrestrial tarantulas use triplines.

Ground-dwelling tarantulas usually line the inside of their burrow with silk and will also spin a thick mat to lie on during the molting process. Male tarantulas in breeding condition use a silk mat to transfer sperm to their pedipalps to ready them for mating. Females lay their eggs in a sack made of spider silk, and tarantulas may use their silk to wrap and store prey items for later feeding.

AMAZING SPIDER SILK

One of the most distinguishing characteristics of the spiders, of course, is their use of silk, which is produced in special glands in their abdomen. A strand of spider silk is several times stronger than a similar-sized strand of hardened steel, and it is more elastic than rubber or any synthetic material.

Mating

Tarantulas have evolved a method of mating that may seem cruel and risky, but has worked well enough to keep these animals thriving for several hundred million years.

Spiderlings.

On reaching maturity, most male tarantulas will develop a thumblike projection near the feet on the first pair of legs, known as the tibial spurs or "mating hooks." (A large number of species, however, do not have these hooks.) The mature male will also develop complicated swollen tips to both pedipalps—these contain a chamber where sperm is stored, and a syringe-like instrument used to insert semen into the female. Once the male has transferred sperm from his genital organs to the tips of his pedipalps, he is ready to reproduce.

For the male tarantula, reproduction is an affair that is fraught with danger. First, in order to find a receptive female spider to mate with, the male tarantula must leave the safety and security of his burrow and wander around until he encounters a female in her shelter. This exposes the male to predators and other dangers. The male must then find a mature female of his own species. Adult females in breeding condition are believed to add chemical signals called pheromones to the silk that lines their shelter. These scents are presumably picked up by the male and allow him to recognize the burrow of a potential breeding partner.

Like all spiders, tarantulas produce silk. Eggsacs are spun from tarantula silk.

Even if the male manages to avoid predators and find a mature female in breeding condition, however, his hazards are still not over. If he is not careful, it is possible that the female tarantula (which is usually larger than the male) may make a meal out of him instead of a mate. Once the male senses the presence of a mature female, he begins a courtship display, which varies from species to species. The female, if receptive, responds with an appropriate display of her own, usually by tapping her feet on the ground. The male's display has two purposes—it signals to the female that the male is here to mate, not to attack (or be eaten), and it ensures that males will most likely mate

DISPARATE LIFE SPANS

Even if the male manages to avoid all of the dangers and mate successfully, he is doomed. Most male tarantulas die of old age within a short time of reaching sexual maturity. The females can live much longer than the males and may be capable of mating for several years once they reach maturity. In its lifetime, a single female tarantula can produce several hundred or even several thousand offspring.

only with their own species, which give the proper courtship signal. In most species, the courtship signal consists of a combination of body vibrations, leg shaking and pedipalp taps.

If the female is receptive to mating, she will turn to face the male and open her fangs. Although this makes her look as if she is giving a threatening display, what she is really doing is exposing the genital opening on the bottom of her abdomen to the male. The male, meanwhile, reaches up to the female with his first pair of legs and grabs both of the female's fangs with his mating hooks, pushing her upwards and allowing him to reach her genital opening with his pedipalps. He carefully inserts the tips of his pedipalps into her genital opening and releases sperm, fertilizing the female. The male will then attempt a hasty retreat, usually escaping his lethal mate. After recharging his pedipalps, the male will be ready to again run the gauntlet and attempt another mating. The female, meanwhile, will construct an eggsac and lay a large number of eggs (from about 80 to over 1,000) within. In most species, she will carry the eggsac around with her and aggressively guard it against any intruders until the spiderlings emerge.

Natural Enemies of the Tarantula

Tarantulas have a whole host of natural enemies that help to keep their population in check. The most widespread of the tarantula's enemies are some of the largest of the living wasps and hornets—the several species of hunting wasps of the *Pepsis* and *Hemipepsis* genera. When the female wasp is ready to lay eggs, she will fly off in search of a tarantula burrow. Once the wasp finds a suitable spider, she entices it out of its shelter and wrestles for position. Her goal is to insert her stinger into the soft underside of the tarantula's cephalothorax. Once the stinger is inserted, the wasp's venom paralyzes the spider. The female wasp will then either drag the immobilized victim to a previously dug burrow, or stuff the spider back into its own tunnel. After laying a single egg on the doomed spider, the wasp will cover up the site and fly off in search of another victim. When the wasp egg hatches, the larva finds itself surrounded by a paralyzed and helpless food source. The larva tunnels its way through the immobilized spider's body, carefully avoiding all of the vital organs until the last moment. Once its growth is complete, the larva pupates and emerges as an adult wasp to begin the cycle over again.

Each species of hunting wasp stalks its own particular species of tarantula. In some species, the method of attack and burial may vary, but the end result is the same—a dead spider and a well-fed wasp grub.

Tarantulas are also attacked by parasitic flies of the subfamily *Panopinae,* the females of which lay eggs near the spider. When the egg hatches, the fly larva crawls up the tarantula's leg and enters the chamber of the booklung. The larva may remain here for several years, until it begins to feed on the spider's internal organs, killing it. After feeding, the larva leaves the spider's body, pupates and emerges as an adult fly. A single tarantula can have over a dozen parasitic fly larvae in its abdomen.

Tarantulas are also parasitized by nematodes or roundworms. These enter the spider's abdomen and grow inside, eventually killing the host. At least one family of spiders, the mimetid pirate spiders, are specialized feeders and eat other spiders almost exclusively, but it is not known whether they are effective predators of young tarantulas.

Even the adult tarantulas are not immune to predators and enemies and are preyed upon by various nocturnal mammals. Although birds are major predators of many spiders, they only rarely eat tarantulas, because birds hunt during the day and tarantulas are largely nocturnal.

Taxonomy and Scientific Names

The science of determining to which classification a particular organism belongs is known as taxonomy. Modern biologists have classified all living things into a hierarchical system, in which organisms are grouped into categories according to their biological traits and characteristics (their "morphology") and also their evolutionary relatedness ("phylogeny"). The basic unit of this classification system is the species, which is usually defined as a population of organisms that are capable of exchanging genetic material and interbreeding to form fertile offspring.

LEVELS OF CLASSIFICATION

A number of species that are closely related to each other through anatomy and evolutionary descent are grouped together in a genus (the plural is genera). Organisms that are more distantly related to each other are grouped at successively higher levels. A group of related genera forms a family, and a group of related families forms an order. The next highest level of classification is the class, and groups of related classes form a phylum (plural is phyla). The largest group of organisms is the kingdom, which consists of several related phyla. If necessary, other categories may be added, such as subfamilies and infraorders. (The *Arthropoda* phylum and the *Araneae* order each contain a number of subgroups.)

SCIENTIFIC NAMES

To distinguish and identify a particular organism, scientists refer to it by its scientific name, consisting of its genus and species designations. Scientific names are usually written in Latin or Greek, and allow scientists from around the world to avoid confusion by assigning a specific name to that organism, regardless of what the varying local names for that animal may be. This Latin name contains the name of the genus and species to which that particular animal has been assigned, and it always refers unequivocally to the same animal. If you refer to a spider that you captured on vacation as an *Aphonopelma chalcodes*, every professional and informed amateur will know exactly to what spider you are referring.

In print, the scientific name is always italicized. Once a particular organism has been referred to by full generic and species name, it can then be shortened in further use to just the first initial followed by the full species name. For instance, now that we have referred above to the full Latin name of the Mexican blonde, we can subsequently refer to its scientific name as *A. chalcodes* without any confusion.

The taxonomic system therefore allows biologists to classify living things in a way that reflects both their unique characteristics and their shared ancestries. The complete classification for the Mexican redknee tarantula, for instance, is:

Kingdom *Animalia:* Multicellular organisms that lack rigid cell walls and have no chloroplasts for photosynthesis. Excludes plants and fungus, includes spiders, insects, crustaceans, snails, fish, reptiles and mammals.

Phylum *Arthropoda:* Animals without backbones, with hard chitinous outer skeletons and multi-jointed limbs. Includes animals such as the spiders, crustaceans, centipedes, millipedes and insects. Excludes all of the vertebrates (fish, reptiles, mammals and birds) as well as many of the invertebrates (including sponges, starfish, squid and clams).

Sub-Phylum *Chelicerata:* Arthropods that possess chelicerae. Includes scorpions, ticks, spiders, the "sea spiders" (which, despite the name, are not really spiders) and the horseshoe crab (which, again, despite the name is not really a crab). Excludes other arthropods including the crustaceans, centipedes, millipedes and insects.

Class *Arachnida:* Chelicerates that possess eight walking legs, and a body with two major divisions. Includes spiders, ticks, scorpions and a number of lesser-known animals. Excludes the horseshoe crab and sea spiders.

Order *Araneae:* Eight-legged arachnids with fangs and spinnerets. Includes spiders. Excludes ticks, scorpions and a few other groups.

Suborder *Ophisthothelae:* Spiders with unsegmented bodies. Includes nearly all of the living spiders. Excludes one living and several extinct primitive segmented families.

Infraorder *Mygalomorphae:* The mygalomorphs. Large hairy spiders with unique structures in their spinnerets and male pedipalps. Includes the tarantulas, trapdoor spiders, purseweb spiders and funnelweb spiders, as well as a few lesser-known families. Excludes all other spiders.

Family *Theraphosidae:* Mygalomorph spiders with hairy bodies and two claws at the end of each foot, each with its own tuft of hair. Includes the tarantulas, excludes all other mygalomorphs, including funnelweb spiders, purseweb spiders and trapdoor spiders.

Subfamily *Theraphosinae:* North and South American terrestrial tarantulas. Includes many of the South American spiders, along with the American *Aphonopelma* and *Brachypelma* species. Excludes a number of other tarantula groups, including the arboreal *Avicularia* species, and the African and Asian tarantulas.

Genus *Brachypelma:* A group of terrestrial tarantulas distinguished by sharing several unique traits in anatomy, particularly in hair construction. Includes the Mexican redknee, Mexican redrump, curly hair tarantulas and a few others. Excludes all other Theraphosines.

Species *smithi:* The particular population of *Brachypelma* spiders found in Mexico, with prominent red or orange markings, which can breed with each other and produce viable offspring.

The classification system tells us about the evolutionary history of this spider as well as its particular physical characteristics. The Mexican redknee is closely related to the other members of the *Brachypelma* genus and shares a recent common ancestor with them. Collectively, the various *Brachypelma* species are all related to the rest of the theraphosids and share a common ancestor with them, while all tarantulas are close evolutionary relatives of the trapdoor spiders and funnelweb spiders. The mygalomorphs are distant relatives of the other spiders and arachnids and share an even more distant evolutionary ancestor with the non-arachnid arthropods. And at the beginning of evolutionary history, the tarantulas share a common ancestor with all multicellular animals.

IDENTIFYING YOUR SPECIES

Although the use of such tongue-twisting Latin designations may seem like a waste of time (or even an exercise in scientific snobbery), it is of vital importance in the tarantula-keeping hobby. Tarantula species vary widely in disposition and sometimes in care requirements.

Many species look superficially alike and are still sold in the pet trade under a bewildering variety of "common names." It may take an expert to accurately determine which species a particular spider is, so the use of Latin scientific names is the only foolproof method to determine exactly what spider you are getting, allowing you to ask particular questions to obtain specific information about the captive husbandry of that species. This is especially important if you plan on handling your spiders. No one should ever attempt to handle any spider, particularly an exotic, that has not been identified. And if you plan on breeding spiders, of course, it is vital that both male and female be accurately identified.

Unfortunately, the number of people who are actively engaged in studying the taxonomy of tarantulas can be counted on the fingers of one hand. Large numbers of spiders remain undescribed, and identification is tortuous and uncertain. Collectors usually consider themselves lucky if they can get an accurate identification to the genus level, and for other arthropods, such as centipedes and millipedes, even a genus identification is unlikely. Many specimens in the pet trade are identified only by a common name (usually one made up by the importer), with either just a genus designation or else no Latin name at all. A vast amount of work remains to be done in this field.

PROBLEMS IN CLASSIFICATION

Scientific names are also changed from time to time as new knowledge of phylogeny is gained, and this often leads to disputes among taxonomists that can be confusing for outsiders. Recently, for instance, the entire large tarantula genus *Brachypelma*, which contains a number of very popular pet spiders, was renamed *Euathlus*, and then very shortly afterwards was renamed *Brachypelma* again (the confusion resulted because someone, decades ago, had mislabeled a specimen bottle). In the past few years, several genera of American spiders, including *Dugesiella* and *Rhechostica*, have been abandoned, and their members have been placed in the large *Aphonopelma* genus. Currently, a dispute is going on about the Latin American *Grammostola* genus (the one containing the common Chilean rose spider), which has now been renamed *Phrixotrichus*. And even this may change yet again.

The popular Mexican redknee tarantula's scientific name is Brachypelna smithi, *or* B. smithi.

There are also disputes over common names and designations. It is not unusual to find the same species of spider being offered by different dealers under several different common names. The species *Brachypelma smithi*, for instance, may be sold as a Mexican redknee, Mexican orangeknee, or Mexican redleg , while the *Brachypelma vagans* species is sometimes sold as the

Mexican redrump and sometimes as the black velvet.
The various large Latin American species are sometimes
referred to collectively as birdeaters, while the large African terrestrials are often referred to as baboon spiders.

Even the name tarantula is under dispute by some
authorities. Because it was originally applied to the
European wolf spider, some experts have argued in
favor of dropping the name tarantula and referring
to the therophosids as mygales, birdeaters or mouse
spiders.

To combat this bewildering variety, a committee within the American Arachnological Society has produced
a standardized list of common names that has been
adopted by the American Tarantula Society (ATS).
Under this list, *B. smithi* is the Mexican redknee, and
B. vagans is the Mexican redrump. The name baboon
properly refers only to the king baboon (*C. crawshayi*),
while the name birdeater should properly be used
only for the Goliath birdeater (*T. blondi*). In practice,
however, the ATS list is not yet completely accepted
(British arachnologists have their own list of common
names). In addition, a number of dealers and writers
continue to use the old names.

Living
with a

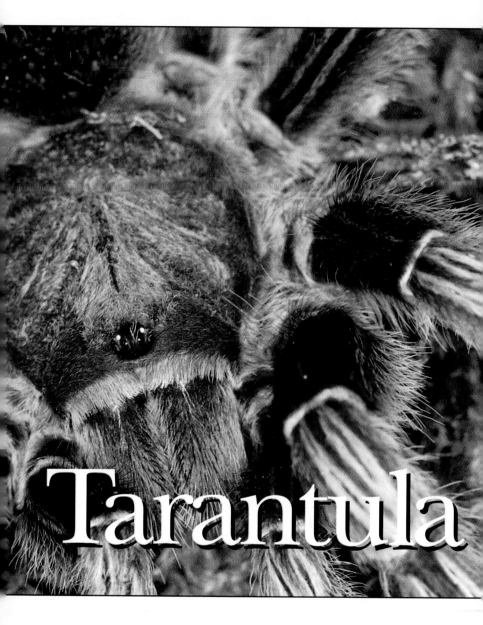

part two

Tarantula

chapter 2

Choosing
a Tarantula

Today, a greater number of tarantula species are available to hobbyists than fifteen years ago. Some of these newly-available species are particularly well-suited for beginners. Other species are more demanding in their requirements and should be kept only by experienced hobbyists. A few tarantula species can be unsafe and dangerous for inexperienced keepers. The species listed below are the ones most commonly seen on dealer lists. They are discussed in approximate order from those most suited for beginners to those appropriate for only experienced keepers.

Spiders Suitable for Beginner and Intermediate Hobbyists

MEXICAN REDKNEE

(*BRACHYPELMA SMITHI*)

Another widely-used common name is Mexican orangeknee. This spider is also sometimes incorrectly referred to as the "Mexican redleg," which more properly refers to the closely related *B. emilia*. The redknee was the first tarantula species to become widely available in the pet trade and is still the one pictured by most people when they hear the word "tarantula."

The jet black body is contrasted sharply by the bright red or orange bands on the joints of the legs and pedipalps. Because they are easy to work with and attractively colored, Mexican redknees are widely used in TV and films, appearing in everything from *James Bond* movies to episodes of *The Brady Bunch*.

Mexican redknee.

These spiders make ideal pets, particularly for beginners. They are hardy, not very demanding in regard to environmental conditions and are the most docile of all the tarantula species. Because of rampant overharvesting from the wild, population levels dropped, and this breed is now listed on international treaties as a threatened species.

An adult Mexican redknee in breeding condition is a very valuable animal. In the wild, where seasonal temperature fluctuations lead to periods of dormancy, these spiders may not be ready to mate until they are 15 years of age; captive animals reach sexual maturity in about five years.

As the common name suggests, the Mexican redknee is native to the coastal regions of Mexico. It is a large spider with a body length of around 2 inches.

If possible, try to obtain a female—although there is no difference in temperament or handleability between the sexes, female tarantulas live, as a rule, much longer than their male counterparts. Some females live up to twenty years.

B. smithi is a terrestrial spider, that prefers hot, dry semidesert terrain. However, because temperatures in the Mexican deserts can drop drastically at night (and because there are seasonal cold spells when the temperature may even drop below freezing), *B. smithi*, like most of the other members of the *Brachypelma* genus, can tolerate a wide range of environmental conditions and temperatures. If it gets too cold, the spider will become inactive and go into a period of hibernation. It should be provided with a daytime temperature in the high 70s and a moderate humidity.

PINKTOE (*AVICULARIA* SPECIES)

The genus name *Avicularia* means "birdeater." This genus was the very first group of tarantulas to be formally scientifically described, back in 1705. The original genus name was *Mygale* (hence the name for the infraorder, *Mygalomorphae*).

Pinktoe.

Although the Latin American group contains some of the largest spiders on earth, the pinktoe is one of the smaller tarantulas. There are actually over a dozen different species in this genus, which range collectively throughout Latin America, available for hobbyists. All have similar habitats and care requirements—which is fortunate, since identifying the members of this genus can be a real task even for an expert. They are all dark colored with pink or reddish patches at the ends of their feet. Spiderlings can have stripes or patterns on the abdomen and pale-colored legs, but lose these as they get older. Some very young spiders reverse the typical adult pattern; instead of being dark

with pink toes, they are pink with dark toes. Pinktoes
have a relatively short life span, with females reaching
ages of 8 or 9 years.

The avics, as they are called, are by far the most common of the arboreal spiders available in the pet trade
(most of the tarantulas kept as pets are terrestrial
burrowers, and not many arboreal species are readily
available). They are adapted for life among the tree
branches, where they spin tubelike webs to hide in.
Avics are astonishing jumpers, capable of leaping from
a considerable height and landing safely on the
ground.

All of the pinktoes are highly prized as pets. They have
a well-deserved reputation for docility (although some
species within the genus can be aggressive) and can
usually be easily and safely handled. They are a bit
jumpy and can be very fast if startled, however, so be
careful that they don't escape from you.

Because they are arboreal, they are better suited for
handling than burrowers, such as the redknee; they are
more surefooted when handled and have a tougher
exoskeleton.

They breed regularly in captivity, and captive-bred
specimens are usually available. The only disadvantage
is that they tend to spend nearly all of their time inside
their webbed retreat and are not often visible.

All of the *Avicularia* species are adapted to life in the
tropical rain forests, so they need daytime temperatures to be in the low 80s, dropping to the high 70s
at night. They also require a somewhat higher humidity than most spiders—at least 75 percent. Their
cage should be lightly misted whenever it dries out.

CHILEAN ROSE (*PHRIXOTRICHUS SPATULATA*)

This widely available spider has largely replaced the
now-endangered Mexican redknee as the beginner's
tarantula of choice. Nearly every pet shop that sells
exotic animals is likely to have one or two of these
spiders for sale. Unfortunately, the Chilean rose does

not breed easily in captivity, and nearly all of the individuals you will find on dealer lists will be captured from the wild. There are some indications that, as with the redknee, the pet trade is reducing the wild population of this spider to dangerously low levels.

Chilean rose.

The genus name was changed recently from *Grammostola,* so you may also see the Chilean rose listed in dealer's catalogues as *Grammostola spatulata.* The rose is a medium-sized spider, reaching a leg span of around 4 inches. As the name suggests, it is native to Chile, where it inhabits dry grassland regions at the edge of the desert. It prefers a moderately high humidity but is more tolerant of drier conditions than most other tarantulas.

The Chilean rose is rather undemanding. Be careful if you plan to handle it, though. Although the rose has a reputation for being docile, it varies widely in individual temperament, and some spiders may be nippy.

CURLYHAIR TARANTULA (*BRACHYPELMA ALBOPILOSUM*)

The curlyhair is closely related to the Mexican redknee and belongs to the same genus. It is a somewhat larger spider, with a leg span of about 5 inches. It is dark brown with a number of long curled hairs lighter in color and scattered over the body and legs.

B. albopilosum is native to Central America. Like the other members of the *Brachypelma* genus, it is a subterranean burrower that either digs its own shelter or sets up house in an abandoned rodent hole. It needs somewhat damper conditions than other spiders in this genus (75 to 80 percent relative humidity), but is not difficult to keep and, though a bit "jumpy," has a reputation for being docile and unaggressive. It lacks the spectacular coloration of the other *Brachypelma* spiders, but is still attractive.

The curlyhair breeds readily in captivity, is inexpensive to obtain and widely available. The only disadvantage is its relatively short life span—males reach sexual maturity at age 2 and die shortly after, while females can live several years after reaching maturity at 3 to 4 years of age.

MEXICAN BLONDE (*APHONOPELMA CHALCODES*)

The Mexican blonde spider is also sometimes sold under the name "palomino tarantula." Its proper common name, according to the American Tarantula Society (ATS) list, is the desert blonde tarantula, but this name has not yet been widely adopted. The carapace and legs are bright gold; the abdomen and feet are darker but flecked with golden hairs.

Mexican blonde.

A. chalcodes is a desert burrowing species that ranges throughout Mexico and the southwestern United States. Like all new-world desert burrowers, it spends nearly all of its time within its silk-lined burrow (which can be as deep as 2 feet), emerging at night to lie in wait for passing prey. During colder months, the spider seals its burrow with a plug of silk and remains inactive until spring.

Closely related species in the *Aphonopelma* genus are found in California and the American Southwest and are sometimes sold under the name "California brown" or "Texas tan." The American *Aphonopelma* species have the longest life spans of any spider, with males often reaching fifteen years of age and females living for forty years or more. Their longevity seems to be related to the fact that they are dormant for part of the year and also to the generally lower temperatures in their home range, which produces a correspondingly lower metabolism.

Like most *Aphonopelma* species, the Mexican blonde has a reputation for being docile and doesn't usually resent handling (although this can vary with the individual spider).

MEXICAN REDRUMP (*BRACHYPELMA VAGANS*)— ALSO KNOWN AS THE "BLACK VELVET"

Mexican redrump.

As the common name suggests, this spider is clothed in glossy black hairs all over the body, with an orange edge to the carapace and a number of longer reddish

hairs on the abdomen. Although it is in the same genus as the more docile *B. smithi* and *B. albopilosum*, it is much more nervous and can act aggressively if it feels threatened. *B. vagans* should be handled carefully, if at all.

The redrump is a terrestrial burrower that is native to the southern parts of Mexico. It has captive husbandry requirements similar to those for *B. smithi* but requires higher humidity.

The redrump breeds easily in captivity and is widely available in the pet trade.

MEXICAN REDLEG (*BRACHYPELMA EMILIA*)

Sometimes also referred to as the "Mexican flameleg" or the "Mexican fireleg," this spider, which is native to the western parts of Mexico, is spectacularly colored, rivaling even the redknee in its beauty. The carapace is a light orange or red with a distinct black V-shaped marking near the eyes, and the abdomen is glossy black with a scattering of longer red or orange hairs. The lower half of the leg (except for the feet) is bright orange or red, which contrasts sharply with the deep black of the upper legs. The redleg does not grow as large as the redknee.

Mexican redleg.

The redleg is a docile spider and usually doesn't resent being handled, but it is unfortunately not widely bred in captivity. Redlegs can be kept in environments similar to those for *B. smithi*, but can also tolerate somewhat drier conditions.

COSTA RICAN ZEBRA (*APHONOPELMA SEEMANNI*)

This large spider reaches a leg span of around 5 inches. It is a terrestrial species, found in the grasslands of Costa Rica, Nicaragua and Panama. It is attractively colored, with a glossy dark brown or black background and a series of short light-colored stripes running down the length of each appendage. It is also sold under the name "stripe knee tarantula."

A. seemanni is a rather hardy spider, and thrives in captivity if provided with proper conditions. It is a dedicated burrower and needs to be provided with a moist substrate for digging. If you provide a short length of tube or some other shelter, it will spend most of its time hidden inside.

The Costa Rican zebra has a relatively short life span for a tarantula—males seldom live more than three years, while females can reach ages of fifteen years.

Although *A. seemanni* is hardy and is suited for a beginner, it is a very nervous spider and can move very fast. Although it does not usually attempt to bite, it is very difficult to control and should not be handled.

Costa Rican zebra.

HAITIAN BROWN (*PHORMICTOPUS CANCERIDES*)

A few years ago, Haitian browns were very common and, along with the redknee, were the staples of the tarantula pet trade. Now, they are seldom imported and are not seen very often on dealer lists. The Haitian brown, as the name suggests, is native to Haiti and the Dominican Republic. It is dark brown with lighter stripes. Males often have a purplish color to the carapace and upper legs.

The Haitian brown is not difficult to care for. It should be provided with warm humid conditions and a substrate suitable for burrowing. *P. cancerides* is an active and fast spider that is usually aggressive. It should not be handled.

Haitian brown.

GREENBOTTLE BLUE (*CROMATOPELMA CYANEOPUBESCENS*)

These gorgeous spiders are, unfortunately, not often found in the pet trade. A terrestrial spider from the scrub areas in northern Venezuela, the greenbottle blue has a shimmering iridescent effect, with varying shades of blue, orange and green.

Unlike most terrestrial spiders, *C. cyaneopubescens* uses silk to construct a large weblike shelter aboveground. It will often web over the entire floor of its cage. Although it requires a rather high humidity level and likes moisture-laden air, the greenbottle blue cannot tolerate damp substrate and must be kept in a well-ventilated cage.

TRINIDAD CHEVRON (*PSALMOPOEUS CAMBRIDGEI*)

The chevron is native to the island of Trinidad, off the coast of Venezuela. The background color on the carapace is dark green, with a striped pattern on the abdomen and bright red stripes on each foot. Males have similar color patterns but sport a number of longer hairs on the legs, which allow the spider to parachute to earth in case of a fall. A large spider, *P. cambridgei* constructs tube webs attached to embankments, walls and tree trunks within which it hides, emerging at night to capture flying insects and other prey.

In captivity, the chevron requires a large vertical tank with a cork board or other surface for building a retreat, and a humidity level of at least 75 percent. There have been some reports that this species has been successfully kept in a communal tank, but the practice is not widespread.

Trinidad chevron.

P. cambridgei is fast and can be aggressive. (Because this breed is one of the few new-world species of tarantula that does not possess urticating hairs, it may be that its increased willingness to bite is an attempt to make up for the lack of this alternative defense mechanism.)

Spiders for More Experienced Hobbyists

The rest of the species discussed here have well-deserved reputations for being aggressive and nasty. All can move very quickly and deliver a painful bite. Some have venom that produces systemic symptoms and should be considered possibly dangerous. These species are not suited for beginning tarantula keepers.

COBALT BLUE (*HAPLOPELMA LIVIDUM*)

The cobalt blue is one of several Asian species that have entered the pet trade only in the past few years. *H. lividum* is native to Thailand and Burma. The females have a grayish body and bright iridescent blue legs, making them a strikingly beautiful and very highly prized spider. Females can reach leg spans of over 5 inches. The males are smaller, with a gold carapace and dark brown legs with lighter stripes.

Like the Latin American tropical species, *H. lividum* needs warm temperatures and high humidity. Daytime temperatures of around 80°F are good, and the humidity should be maintained at about 80 percent. The substrate must be misted every day.

The cobalt blue is a shy species that prefers to remain hidden in its burrow. If threatened, however, it will defend itself aggressively. It is not suitable for handling, even by experienced keepers. As a result, the cobalt blue is not a very good choice for beginners.

Cobalt blue.

GOLIATH BIRDEATER (*THERAPHOSA BLONDI*)

Also known as the Brazilian birdeater, *T. blondi* is one of the largest species of spider alive today, with a leg span reaching an incredible 10 inches or more. Although rather dull in appearance (a uniform dark brown in color with faint markings on the legs), its large size makes it a spectacular display animal, and it is often found in zoo collections. It has largely replaced the Mexican redknee as a Hollywood favorite.

T. blondi is a terrestrial burrower that is usually found inhabiting rodent burrows and other makeshift shelters. Adult Goliath spiders are fully capable of overpowering and eating small rodents, as well as snakes, lizards, frogs, small birds and other tarantulas.

THINGS TO LOOK FOR

If you don't plan to handle your spider, it won't make any difference if it is aggressive. If you do plan to handle it, however, make sure the individual spider is relatively passive before you purchase it.

If the spider that you examine has a little hook on the inside of each front leg, it is an adult male in mating condition. Adult males should be avoided as pets—they die within a year of reaching sexual maturity. As far as longevity goes, the very best pet is an immature female, which in some species can live as long as forty years.

In captivity, *T. blondi* requires very humid conditions, at least 85 percent humidity, in addition to tropical temperatures in the 80s. Captive breeding is not particularly common, but spiderlings are sometimes available.

Goliath birdeater.

The Goliath belongs to one of several genera of tarantula in which the males lack the tibial spurs or "mating hooks" found on most theraphosids.

The Goliath birdeater is one of the many tarantulas that uses an auditory warning if it feels threatened. The stridulatory process of *T. blondi* is unique—it consists of a number of hairs on the pedipalps and forelegs that form a series of tiny hooks and loops, like Velcro. These are rubbed together to produce the warning sound.

The urticating hairs of *T. blondi* are also extremely irritating and can produce a severe rash. In addition, the Goliath is nervous and aggressive and can deliver a bad bite, which sometimes produces systemic symptoms in the victim, including nausea. It is not a spider for beginners.

TOGO STARBURST (*HETEROSCODRA MACULATA*)

The Togo starburst is one of several African species of tarantula that have been recently introduced to collectors. The starburst is native to rain forests in Togo and Benin. The common name refers to the attractive radiated pattern found on the carapace. *H. maculata* is widely captive-bred. The males in this genus, along with several others, are unusual among tarantulas in lacking the tibial mating spurs found in most genera.

The Togo starburst is an arboreal species that builds a webbed retreat in the canopy, sometimes as high as 40 feet from the ground. Unlike most arboreal spiders, the starburst has rather short legs but can still move quickly and is an excellent jumper. It is very aggressive and bites readily; this makes it difficult to control. Its venom is reported to have systemic effects. It is best left to experienced spider keepers.

Togo starburst.

KING BABOON (*CITHARISCHIUS CRAWSHAYI*)

The king baboon is one of the largest of the African spiders, with a leg span approaching 8 inches. Its natural habitat is the dry veldt or savanna areas in Kenya and Tanzania, where it prefers to make a burrow near the base of the large acacia trees that dot the landscape. The spider will ambush prey as it walks by the burrow, and can tackle even vertebrate prey, such as rodents and small reptiles.

This King baboon is devouring a mouse.

In captivity, *C. crawshayi* prefers somewhat drier conditions than its rain forest cousins, with a humidity level of around 50 percent. It is not being captive-bred in the United States.

51

Like all of the African species, *C. crawshayi* is nervous and aggressive. Although somewhat clumsy on land, it can move rapidly in its burrow. It is suited only as a display animal; and even then, only by experienced keepers.

CAMEROON RED (*HYSTEROCRATES GIGAS*)

Another member of the African group of tarantulas, the Cameroon red is a terrestrial spider that builds extensive burrows in the damp rain forest floor. As the Latin name indicates, it is a very large spider, with leg spans of up to 6 inches.

Cameroon red.

In the wild, the Cameroon red prefers moist areas near water, and in captivity it requires high humidity levels of up to 90 percent. *H. gigas* will spend nearly all of its time in its burrow, emerging occasionally at night while waiting for prey to wander by.

The males of this species lack the tibial spurs found in other groups. *H. gigas* breeds regularly in captivity though, and spiderlings are widely available.

This spider is extremely aggressive and bites readily. One tarantula keeper described it aptly as "meaner than a wet cat." It stridulates using hairs between the first and second pair of legs.

Hercules Tarantula
(*Hysterocrates hercules*)

The largest spider in Africa, *H. hercules*, also sometimes known as the African Goliath, reaches leg spans in excess of 9 inches. It is a terrestrial burrower, but prefers a much more humid climate than most of its African cousins. Also, like most of the African spiders, it is bad-tempered, easily provoked and will bite aggressively.

There is some dispute as to whether the spiders sold in the United States under this name are actually members of the *H. hercules* species, or whether they represent a different but related species.

Mombasa Starburst
(*Pterinochilus murinus*)

One of the most widely available of the African species, the Mombasa starburst is a large terrestrial burrower. It is reddish brown, with darker appendages and markings on the abdomen and carapace. *P. murinus* is native to the savanna regions of eastern Africa. It can tolerate much drier conditions than other spiders, as long as it is allowed to burrow.

The Mombasa starburst is fast, aggressive and will bite without warning. It also stridulates readily at any perceived threat. Its venom is reported to have systemic effects, and it should be considered potentially dangerous.

Usumbara orange, a member of the Pterinochilus *genus.*

In addition to the Mombasa, other members of the *Pterinochilus* genus (usually more orangish in color) are also widely available, usually under the name "Usumbara orange" or "Usumbara red."

None are suitable for beginners.

HORNED TARANTULA
(*CERATOGYRUS* SPECIES)

There are seven species of horned tarantula in this genus, all of them from dry areas of Africa. In the past, they were very rare in the pet trade but are now becoming more widely available. The species seen most often in captivity are *C. darlingi* and *C. cornuatus*. Adults range in size from 3½ to 5 inches in leg span.

Cranial Horned Baboon (C. Cornuatus).

As the name suggests, these unusual tarantulas are distinguished by a hornlike projection, looking something like a shark's fin, on the back of the carapace. Very young spiders have no horn (it begins to develop when the spider reaches 1 or 2 inches in leg span). One theory is that the horn provides attachment places for additional muscles for the sucking stomach, allowing the spider to digest prey with a very low moisture content. Male spiders have smaller horns than females.

The *Ceratogyrus* spiders require dry, well-ventilated conditions. They should be provided with a deep, dry substrate, a piece of bark for a shelter and a shallow water dish for drinking. Some spiders will burrow extensively; others will web over the inside of the cage instead. Like most African species, they are very fast and can be aggressive, stridulating at any disturbance. They should not be handled.

INDIAN ORNAMENTAL (*POECILOTHERIA REGALIS*)

One of the few Asian spiders to enter the pet trade, the Indian ornamental (also sometimes referred to as the "poke") is a strikingly beautiful spider, with an attractive black and white pattern and a splash of bright yellow under the forelegs. Although it is an arboreal tarantula, it rarely builds an extensive webbed shelter like other tree-dwellers, preferring instead to utilize cavities and other ready-made retreats off the ground. The males lack the tibial mating spurs found in most other tarantulas.

When young, the ornamentals are communal and have even been observed feeding from the same prey item. Some keepers have had success maintaining adult *P. regalis* in large communal cages—others who have tried it ended up with one very well-fed spider.

Although the poke makes a wonderful display animal, it is probably the most dangerous species of tarantula kept in captivity. It is extremely aggressive, fast and is a good leaper and climber. Although most specimens will run away if disturbed, this breed is capable of defending itself vigorously if it feels threatened—and they always feel threatened. The venom is also particularly powerful, and produces weakness, cramps and other systemic reactions that can require hospitalization. It is not a spider for the inexperienced.

Indian ornamental.

TRAPDOOR SPIDERS

The trapdoor spiders, of the family *Ctenizidae*, are not true tarantulas, but they are mygalomorphs and are closely related to the theraphosids. In appearance they are very similar to tarantulas, but are distinguished by some anatomical details in the feet and claws. For the most part, trapdoor spiders are much less hairy than the true tarantulas, and they tend to be more drab in color. They are also smaller and have relatively shorter legs. Most of these anatomical differences are the result of their increased specialization for a burrowing existence.

Trapdoor spiders are more widespread than tarantulas and can tolerate a wider range of environmental conditions. In the United States, they are found as far north as Ohio. Many of those found on dealer lists are imported from Africa.

All of the trapdoor spiders have nasty dispositions and are *extremely* aggressive. They should never be handled. Although they are not difficult to care for in captivity, one serious disadvantage to keeping them as pets is their extreme subterranean lifestyle. Trapdoor spiders must be given sufficient substrate for burrowing or they will die. They will dig a burrow and cap it with a hinged lid, made from dirt and soil cemented with silk. The trapdoor spider then waits near the top of the burrow until it feels the vibrations of a passing prey animal, whereupon it pops open the door, reaches out with its fangs, seizes its prey and drags it back inside.

Once it has constructed a suitable shelter, you will probably never see your trapdoor spider again—except for a brief instant when it reaches from its burrow to snap up a passing prey animal. Even the "trapdoor" is hard to see unless you know where it is. For the most part, your trapdoor spider tank will look like nothing at all is living in it.

How to Obtain a Tarantula
BREEDERS AND HOBBYISTS

As with most exotic pets, it is far preferable to obtain a spider that was captive-bred rather than one caught in the wild. One of the best ways to obtain a pet tarantula is through a local breeder or collector, someone who breeds a small number of tarantulas as a hobby. The advantages to this method are numerous: Most

noncommercial local tarantula breeders are very con-
scientious about their animals and take extraordinary
care in keeping and caring for them (if they didn't,
they would have no spiderlings to sell). Because the
breeder has a wealth of experience in keeping and raising a particular species, he or she will be able to answer
any questions that you have and pass on useful information and tips on caring for your spider. Price-wise,
most noncommercial private breeders are competitive
with mail-order dealers, without the shipping costs.

There are, however, a few disadvantages as well, and
they must be carefully considered. The biggest problems in dealing with noncommercial breeders are finding one (as noncommercial tarantula breeders are
very rare) and lack of variety. (Breeding tarantulas
takes a lot of space and some expenditure of money—
for this reason, most private breeders tend to specialize
in one, or a small number of species.)

Most breeders prefer to sell their stock soon after it is
born. This means that when you buy from a breeder,
you will probably be dealing with spiderlings. As far as
husbandry requirements go, spiderlings are not very
different from their adult counterparts—they are simply smaller (sometimes much smaller; most spiderlings
are scarcely ½ inch in leg span when sold) and a bit
more delicate. Because they are so tiny, they lose moisture rapidly and dry out much more easily than adult
spiders, and therefore require more humid conditions.

Finding appropriately-sized food for such tiny predators can also be a problem, although a colony of fruit
flies or baby "pinhead" crickets will guarantee a steady
supply of prey.

Spiderlings are a bit more work than adults; they shed
much more often and must be fed every other day or
so, but many tarantula keepers find the process of
raising a tarantula from a width smaller than a dime to
a dinner-plate–sized adult to be enjoyable and fasci-
nating. From an economic point of view, spiderlings
are much less expensive than adults, and from a
conservationist point of view they reduce the need to

take animals from the wild. Captive-bred spiderlings are also much less likely to carry parasites.

One disadvantage, though, is that you will not be able to choose the sex of your spider, since it is virtually impossible to tell a male from a female until the spider reaches sexual maturity. Remember, male tarantulas have much shorter life spans than females and will die shortly after reaching sexual maturity.

By far, the most versatile way to obtain a pet tarantula is through a mail-order dealer or commercial breeder. Moreover, for some of the more exotic tarantulas, this may be the only source for that species. (Contact information for several tarantula dealers is listed in chapter 8.)

The first step in obtaining a tarantula through mail order is to decide what species you would like, and then to write to the dealer for a price list in order to ensure that he or she has it. Because tarantulas may be sold under several different names in the pet trade, most dealer lists will give the scientific name in addition to the common name. To ensure that you get the exact species you want, use the scientific name when you place your order.

In general, you can expect to pay about half as much for a dealer's tarantula as you would in the pet store. A tarantula that would sell for around $20 in a pet shop, for example, would appear on a dealer's list for about $10. In addition to this price, however, you will need to pay the shipping and handling. Most spiders can be safely shipped by priority mail, which is inexpensive but takes a few days. Some people prefer to have their spiders shipped overnight or by airmail, which is much faster but costs more.

Any reputable dealer will guarantee live arrival of your tarantula. Once you get your package, you should open it immediately to check the condition of your tarantula. If there is a problem, you must contact the dealer immediately. Only a very tiny percentage of shipped tarantulas do not survive the trip. Your dealer will probably request that you send some verification of the tarantula's condition (most will accept a photograph of the dead tarantula resting on a current newspaper as sufficient proof). He or she will then ship you another tarantula.

PET SHOPS

Most people, particularly beginners in the hobby, obtain their first spider at the local pet shop. The pet store gives you the opportunity to examine any tarantulas that you are interested in before you buy them. The disadvantages are that you will probably pay more in a pet shop than you would to a dealer, and your selection will be limited to the species that the pet shop has available. It may also be difficult to get an accurate identification of a pet shop tarantula.

Pet Shop Warning Signs

Even an untrained eye can quickly pick out some danger signals that should steer you away from a store where the employees know little about tarantulas or where the animals are kept under poor conditions. Do the cages look clean and well-maintained, or do they have dirty substrate, empty water dishes and no heat source? Tarantulas kept in dirty, ill-maintained cages are likely to develop mites and other health problems later on.

HERP SHOWS

Another way to obtain a tarantula is through a breeder at one of the various herp shows that are held around the country. These are frequented by breeders and collectors of reptiles and amphibians (known collectively to insiders as herps), but a number of tarantula breeders also make the rounds. The advantage that these shows have over mail-order dealers is that you won't have to pay any shipping costs, and you will be able to see and examine any spider before you buy it. Also, at these shows, you will be able to talk firsthand with someone who has experience with a particular species, and who can pass on information about care and keeping

3

Housing
Your
Tarantula

There are a variety of ways to house captive tarantulas. None is very expensive, and none require any large amounts of space or equipment.

The particular housing method to be used depends on the particular species to be kept, how old and how large the spider is and whether or not you intend to handle the tarantula or use it in talks or shows.

Cohabitation

One rule applies to nearly all captive spiders—with only one possible exception, all tarantulas must be housed alone in individual cages. Tarantulas are not social animals, and in the wild they spend their whole lives alone in a burrow or shelter, away from members of their own or other species. If housed together, the larger spider will sooner or later attack, overpower and eat its cagemate.

The *Poecilotheria* species can often be found living near one another in the wild (*Poecilotheria* spiders will actually share shelters), and some keepers have successfully maintained *Poecilotheria* in communal tanks. Although there have been some reports of keepers attempting to house *Avicularia* spiders together (making sure each spider has enough space for its own individual shelter), all of these attempts appear to have been unsuccessful, as cannibalism usually results when the spiders find each other's retreats.

Although a large planted vivarium containing a number of the social spiders can be breathtakingly beautiful, it requires a lot of attention and is not recommended for beginning spider keepers.

Burrowers and Arboreals

Tarantulas fall into two basic ecological categories: burrowers and arboreals. Burrowers live in holes in the ground—holes they've either dug themselves or appropriate from other animals. Arboreals construct their own silken shelters on trees, rock faces or the sides of buildings.

While the environmental needs of both kinds of tarantula are basically the same, housing needs for burrowers differ slightly from those of arboreal climbing species.

Cage Size

Tarantulas are generally inactive animals that spend nearly all of their time sitting placidly at the entrance to their shelters and, therefore, do not require a lot of room and can thrive in surprisingly small accommodations. For most average-sized tarantulas, a 5-gallon or even a 2½ gallon tank is plenty large. The

> **FLYING THE COUP**
>
> When housing *any* tarantula, a number of factors must be kept in mind. Tarantulas are superb escape artists. The arboreal species and many terrestrial species are usually capable of climbing straight up the sides of their cage, even a glass tank. Even the clumsiest of terrestrial burrowers can lay a fine mesh of silk against the side of its tank, which it will use to climb up and out.
>
> All tarantula housing must therefore have a securely fitting lid.

rough rule of thumb is to make the cage about twice as wide as the leg span of the spider and about three times as long. Tanks for burrowing species should not be any deeper from top to substrate than the length of the spider. Arboreal cages should be larger to provide more space, and can be as tall as you would like to make them.

Types of Housing

AQUARIUMS

The most common housing used for captive tarantulas are ordinary tropical fish aquariums. These have the advantages of being cheap and readily available. They also hold humidity well and allow you to have a good view of your pet. But, there are several disadvantages to aquariums as spider cages, and some of these present real dangers to the animal.

Tarantulas are great escape artists—don't make it easier for them!

Because the sides of aquarium tanks are so high, they represent potential danger to burrowing spiders, who may attempt to climb up the inside of the tank, resulting in a fall. Remember, to a terrestrial tarantula, a fall of even 6 inches can be deadly.

Another disadvantage to the glass aquarium is that it provides little security. Finding a secure lid that is also safe for the spider will be difficult. The plastic fluorescent hoods that are available for fish tanks are not suitable for keeping tarantulas. They usually have a number of holes for air lines, filters and other apparatus, and thus offer many potential avenues of escape. Because it cannot usually be locked into place, the large door that opens to allow feeding is also a security problem. Even if held by tape, these doors are not difficult for a determined spider to pry open.

TANK LIDS

Screen Lids

Screen lids for the most common aquarium sizes are widely available in pet shops. However, these are intended for housing small animals and reptiles, and are not very well-suited for tarantulas. The most popular lids, which consist of a metal frame and screen, held in place by small metal springs, present several safety hazards to the spider.

The first danger is that the sharp wire screen will damage the exoskeleton and result in bleeding—a serious matter for any tarantula. The second potential threat is the possibility that the

All tarantula cages need securely locking lids to prevent escapes.

spider will, during its wandering and climbing, get stuck in a position where it will be hanging free from the lid by the claws of one or two legs. The spider will not have sufficient leverage to lift its claws and get down, and hence it will be trapped there until it either dies or is released.

Metal Lids

A second type of aquarium lid that is sometimes available consists of a perforated sheet of thin, flexible metal with a knob at either end that hooks a metal tongue under the lip of the tank to hold it in place. Because the holes are much smaller and there are no sharp wires anywhere, these are safer for the spider than ordinary screen lids, but they present security problems of their own. There are no fasteners at the sides of these lids and spiders have been known to bend the metal and create an opening at this point, through which they can squeeze underneath and escape.

SWEATER BOXES

Given all of the problems that can result from using fish tanks, an alternative option should be considered. Housing terrestrial burrowing spiders in the clear or translucent plastic boxes with snap-on lids that are commonly used for storing sweaters seems to be the ideal way. These sweater boxes can be found almost anywhere, and come in a wide range of sizes and shapes. For all but the largest species, the common 8-quart size, measuring approximately 18 × 12 × 6 inches, is perfect.

Using sweater boxes as housing can help you save space.

These sweater boxes offer several advantages over aquariums. They come with their own lids that fit perfectly and snap securely into place. There are no screens, holes or other potential avenues of escape. The sides of the tank are very low and present no danger of falling for terrestrial spiders. The wide box and low sides offer easy access to the keeper for cleaning and cage maintenance. They also make it easy to transfer fast and aggressive spiders from one cage to another.

Sweater boxes are particularly well-suited for keepers who maintain large collections. Because these boxes stack on top of one another, they allow hobbyists to keep a large number of cages in a limited space. It is also possible to buy or construct rack systems to hold a large number of these cages. In some rack systems, the lidded cages fit onto a number of shelves. In other systems, the individual cages have no lids, but instead slide in snugly and use the bottom of the shelf above as the lid. For easiest handling of fast-moving species, the lidded systems are preferable.

Before they can be turned into suitable cages for tarantulas, however, plastic sweater boxes need to be modified slightly. Tarantulas do not require large amounts of oxygen, but they do need at least a small amount of air flow, which must be provided through air holes. Also, good ventilation is a necessity in tanks housing tropical spiders, particularly arboreals, because the combination of high humidity and stagnant air will lead to all sorts of mold and fungus infestations. Therefore, a number of air holes should be provided for ventilation.

One type of sweater box is made from hard, clear plastic. The more common type of box is made from a softer, translucent plastic. To create holes in either type of box, use an electric soldering tool to melt them in. You can also perform this task by carefully heating a Phillips tip screwdriver over the stove.

Caging Tarantulas that You Will Be Handling

Tarantulas that are to be handled regularly should be maintained in a utilitarian cage without a burrow or shelter to ease the process of removing and handling the spider. They tend to treat cages as enormous burrows and will line the cages with silk, usually making no effort to construct their own shelters.

It is extremely important to keep the utilitarian-style cages scrupulously clean; if the substrate becomes littered with dirt, food remains and dead prey animals, the warmth and dampness will provide perfect conditions for mites, fungus and other parasites. Only a few species, including the Chilean rose and the Mexican redknee, should be kept in such spartan housing.

Natural Cages

Most tarantulas should be housed under natural conditions, with shelters or burrows, in order to reduce stress on the spider and to allow it to exhibit its natural behavior patterns. A row of air holes just under the lid and another row along the bottom of the cage will be sufficient. The spider will usually construct a web retreat or burrow in order to escape the higher air flow and to provide an area of locally high humidity.

Tarantulas living under natural conditions rarely leave their shelters except at night, so this type of cage should not be used if you intend to handle the spider. Some of the more delicate species, however, must have a suitable shelter if they are to survive, and these spiders can only be kept in a naturalistic cage.

Critter Cages

Many spiders are sold in small plastic containers known as critter cages. These can serve as acceptable alternatives to the plastic sweater box cage, provided the cage is of proper size and the lid is secure (many of these setups have little latches that hold the lid on securely).

A disadvantage of these cages is the plastic screening found on the lid, which can result in too much air flow and make it difficult to keep a proper level of humidity. If necessary, the humidity in these cages can be raised by placing tape over most of the lid openings.

Housing for Arboreal Spiders

Arboreal species, such as pinktoes, Trinidad chevrons or Indian ornamentals, require somewhat special housing. Because these species rarely descend to the ground, they require tanks that provide a maximum amount of vertical space for climbing and not much ground surface area. However, larger plastic cages provide enough vertical space for an arboreal spider. Another option is to use a plastic food container with a sealable lid of appropriate size and height. This must also include a number of ventilation holes similar to those in the sweater boxes.

Although arboreal spiders generally prefer a higher humidity level than their terrestrial cousins, these modified cages nevertheless require a large number of air holes to provide sufficient ventilation and prevent stagnant air. The cage will need to be misted with water often to keep the humidity acceptably high (see the section on humidity later in this chapter).

AQUARIUMS

It is also possible to use a small aquarium, placed upright on one end to provide the proper vertical space, but this setup will present all of the security problems found with aquarium screen lids.

One potential problem that you will run into with arboreal spiders is that they will ordinarily construct their own retreats out of silk. These are built in the most protected spot—usually an upper corner of the tank, next to the lid. This often makes it impossible to open the cage without destroying the webbed shelter. This can usually be prevented by placing sticks or tree bark to form a sheltered spot high in the cage.

Most often, the spider will then choose to make its retreat in this protected spot instead of against the lid. If the shelter is repeatedly built in an inconvenient spot, you will simply have to keep destroying it. Eventually the spider will give up and move to another spot.

Housing Spiderlings

Housing for spiderlings is a bit different from that for adult or subadult spiders. Very small cages are a necessity, both to allow the keeper to easily find the spiderling and to ensure that the young spider will be able to find the food-animals placed in its enclosure. The humidity level necessary for keeping a young spiderling is also much higher than that which is needed for an older tarantula.

Hatchling spiders are very small and usually have a leg span of less than $\frac{1}{2}$ inch. These tiny arachnids can be kept in rather small containers, which allow you to maintain the necessary high humidity levels and make it easier for a young spiderling to find and capture the provided prey animals. Baby food jars make good homes for very young spiderlings. Some keepers have raised hatchlings in the clear, round plastic containers that hold rolls of 35mm film. Other containers, including the vials that hold prescription pills and the plastic tubes that are used to raise fruit flies, can also be used after having been thoroughly washed and provided with ventilation holes.

Deli Cups

The containers mentioned above can present some problems, however. Because they are tall and have a narrow base, they can be easily knocked over. They also

Pictured are different types of containers that can be used to house spiderlings.

have limited surface area, which may be okay for arboreal climbers, but can leave terrestrial spiders a bit cramped.

The best homes for spiderlings are made from clear plastic deli cups with tight-fitting lids—the kind used to package fresh fruit or pasta salad. These are available in several sizes and provide enough space for a young burrowing or arboreal tarantula. A number of ventilation holes should be melted through the lid (be very careful that these are not large enough to allow the spiderling to escape).

Most cages for housing spiderlings should be empty of furniture and decoration; they should contain only a layer of suitable substrate that is deep enough for burrowing. This is also true of the utilitarian-type cage for terrestrial spiders. Cages for subadult and larger arboreal tarantulas and naturalistic cages for burrowers will require additional cage furniture.

Humidity

Humidity is an important factor to watch when housing any species of tarantula. All spiders, even those from the most harsh desert regions, constantly lose moisture through their booklungs and require a minimum level of humidity to prevent them from drying

out and to ensure that exoskeletons can be shed safely
and completely. If the humidity levels are insufficient,
particularly during a molt, the spider can be killed.
Hatchlings and young spiderlings need higher humidity levels than their larger counterparts.

Tropical rain forest species, both terrestrial and arboreal, are adapted to high humidity levels in the air.
Desert species receive their required humidity levels
by digging a deep burrow or shelter, which traps the
moisture present in the soil and provides a locally high
area of humidity. For the most part, tarantulas prefer to have humid air and a dry substrate. The exact
environmental conditions depend on the particular
species.

The utilitarian cage does not allow the spider to burrow, hence the required level of humidity must be
maintained throughout the entire cage. This is best accomplished by both providing a proper water dish
and by using a proper substrate that is misted when it
dries out.

Misting can be carried out with a small spray bottle
or atomizer, which can be found in any beauty supply
or garden shop. The substrate should be squirted two
or three times until it is damp. Do not spray water
directly onto the spider; it will react defensively to this
annoyance.

Naturalistic cages for terrestrial burrowers can be
somewhat drier than the spartan utilitarian enclosures
but still require at least a moderately high moisture
level. The webbing at the mouth of the burrow or shelter should be misted daily, and a shallow water dish
should always be available.

USING PLANTS TO MAINTAIN HUMIDITY

Keeping live plants in the cage can also help maintain
proper humidity. These can be rooted in small pots,
which should be buried in the substrate up to the rim.
The plants will not be harmed by the spider (though
the spider may choose to construct its silken shelter

among the leafs), but be sure to pick a species of plant that can tolerate conditions of low light and high humidity. Snake plants do well, have long tough leaves suitable for shelter and are good choices for planting in an arboreal tarantula cage.

Despite the help plants provide in maintaining humidity, most keepers do without them, as it is extremely difficult to keep them alive under these conditions.

SUBSTRATE

Nearly all of the tarantulas found in pet stores are kept on a substrate of dry sand or aquarium gravel. In most cases, this is a misguided attempt to duplicate the conditions that most people associate with these animals. Tarantulas are usually thought of as desert animals, so many keepers mistakenly keep them in dry substrates (such as sand), which fail to provide the proper humidity levels. Being kept in conditions that are too dry is probably the leading cause of death among captive tarantulas.

Despite the temptation to emulate the desert, tarantulas should not be kept on sand or gravel.

Vermiculite

There are two basic types of substrate that are suitable for a tarantula's cage. Both have their supporters and their detractors, but both have been used successfully by many keepers to maintain their tarantulas. The first type consists of a substance called vermiculite. This is made by subjecting the mineral mica to high temperatures, causing it to become fluffy and absorbent. Vermiculite is commonly used in gardening to condition the soil for potted plants and can usually be obtained inexpensively in any garden supply shop. It is available in several sizes or grades. The medium grade is best for adult spiders, and the fine grade is suitable for spiderlings.

Although some people find its appearance unattractive, vermiculite is dust- and odor-free, holds moisture well and resists infestation by mites or other parasites. One drawback is that it doesn't hold its shape very well and is therefore difficult for the tarantula to form burrows in. It is probably the substrate of choice for utilitarian cages, in which spiders will be maintained without a burrow. It is also ideal for arboreal species, as they do not often descend to the ground anyway. (Some keepers prefer not to use any substrate at all in their arboreal spider cages.) Simply line the bottom of the cage with an inch or so of vermiculite and spray it until it is damp.

Mixture Substrate

Naturalistic cages that will house burrowing species require a different substrate. The best option is a mixture of several different materials. A strong combination is one part sterile potting soil with one part peat moss. Both of these materials are widely available in garden supply shops. This mixture holds dampness well and seems to be easy for burrowers to tunnel into.

> ### SUBSTRATES TO AVOID
>
> In addition to sand or aquarium gravel, there are some other substances that should be avoided in a tarantula's cage. Cedar and pine oils are very toxic to all arthropods, and materials such as pine shavings and cedar chips should never be used for captive spiders. Other materials to avoid are newspaper, ground up corn cob and commercial bedding made from recycled paper, as these cannot provide proper levels of moisture and tend to get moldy when damp.
>
> Bark or wood chips also provide good hiding and breeding places for mites, which hitchhike their way into the cage on crickets and other prey animals.

If you have problems with the burrow collapsing, add a few handfuls of bark mulch—the very small chips sold as orchid bark work best—to the mixture. These will be webbed into place by the spider and will help provide support and cohesion. A thin layer of bark atop the soil will also improve the appearance and help keep the substrate damp for tropical species that prefer high humidity.

Desert tarantulas and those from arid savannah regions prefer a somewhat drier substrate. For desert species, replace the peat moss mixture with a mix of fifty-fifty potting soil and washed playground sand.

This substrate is crumbly and usually needs a few hand-fuls of orchid bark to make burrowing easier.

These substrates should be at least 4 or 5 inches deep at the bottom of the cage to allow sufficient room for the tarantula to construct a burrow. The substrate should be damp, but not so wet that it does not crumble apart easily if squeezed in the hand. If you can squeeze a handful of substrate and it holds the shape of your hand, it is too damp. Wet substrates will attract parasites and fungus, causing the cage to become infested and smell bad.

This adult Chilean rose is being kept in a utilitarian cage with a vermiculite substrate. (Notice the wire for the heater.)

Heating

Tarantulas are ectotherms, and so they will become inactive at lower temperatures. Therefore, they must be provided with sufficient heat to maintain their body temperature at a suitable level. Most species will need temperatures to fall between 75° and 80°F. Desert animals live in places where the temperature can top 100°F during the day and then drop below freezing at night, but they always remain in their burrows, where the temperature and humidity remain at acceptable levels during these temperature extremes.

The simplest way to provide proper temperature for your tarantula is to keep the room it is kept in at room temperature—the preferred temperature for most tarantulas. If you have a large spider collection with a number of cages, this will allow you to avoid the necessity of providing separate heat sources for each cage.

If you keep tropical spiders and you live in an area that gets cold in the winter, you may need to provide some source of supplemental heat. American species of tarantula, and many of the Mexican ones as well, will simply become inactive through the cold winter months and begin feeding again in the spring.

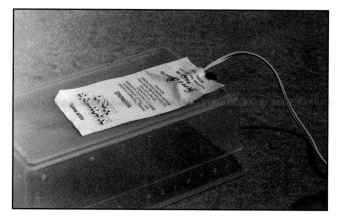

Undertank heaters attach directly to the bottom of the tank, providing heat.

If you have a number of cages that need to be heated, you might consider placing them all in a much larger enclosure that can itself be heated. This works particularly well with spiderlings—just fill a large aquarium with a substrate of 2 inches of damp vermiculite and arrange the spiderling containers on top of this. Heat can be provided either by placing an incandescent spotlight above the cage or by placing a commercial undertank heater on the aquarium. The undertank heater (which looks like a little electric blanket and was designed to assist in keeping reptiles) attaches to the bottom of the tank and is heated electrically. The heat diffuses through the substrate and warms the cage. This arrangement helps provide proper heat and humidity for the developing spiderlings. The substrate will have to be sprayed every day to keep it damp.

Lighting

Nearly all tarantula species are nocturnal and spend the daylight hours in their burrow or shelter. Even the arboreal tropical rain forest species live in an environment where sunlight is filtered through a canopy of leaves and levels of ambient light are very low. As a result, captive tarantulas need subdued lighting. Bright lights stress out tarantulas and should be avoided. Ordinary room lighting levels are suitable for all species, and no light sources are needed for the cage itself. If a light bulb is used as an external heat source, it should be blue or red. These wavelengths are invisible to spiders, and the tarantula will behave as if it were dark.

Shelters and Hiding Places

A few tarantulas, such as the Goliath birdeater, will make use of a suitable shelter if one is available instead of constructing a burrow. A wide variety of shelters can be provided for spiders that do not want to dig their own. A small cave made from flat pieces of rock (secured into place with silicone aquarium sealer) can serve as a retreat. Some keepers simply break a clay flowerpot in half and use each piece as a shelter. Burying short lengths of PVC pipe in the substrate with one end protruding at ground level to form a sort of artificial burrow also works.

Sustenance Dishes and Cage Furniture

Water Dish

The most important accessory you will need for your tarantula's cage is a water dish. Although tarantulas get most of the moisture they need from their prey, they can and do drink water that is not running, and all captive tarantulas, even those from desert areas, require access to clean drinking water at all times. (The only exception to this is when dealing with small spiderlings. Because spiderlings require a much higher humidity level than adult tarantulas and therefore a much damper substrate, they will be able to drink enough water right from the damp soil or vermiculite to meet their needs.)

Water can be provided in any shallow dish that is heavy enough not to be tipped over (glass furniture coasters or ashtrays work well). A tarantula's mouth is located on the underside of its cephalothorax, so in order to drink, it is necessary for the spider to place its whole face in the water dish. For this reason, the dish needs to be shallow, with sides low enough for the spider to reach the water. For arboreal spiders, make the water dish as large as practical to help keep the humidity high.

OTHER WATERING OPTIONS

Most pet shops place sponges in the water dish in order for the spider to be able to suck moisture from the surface of the sponge when it needs it. While this prevents crickets from falling in and drowning (dead crickets smell awful, make a mess and attract parasites), sponges also tend to attract parasites, and are therefore not an ideal water source. A healthier option is to fill the water dish with pebbles so that the crickets can climb out.

ARBOREAL FURNITURE

Arboreal spiders require an additional piece of furniture in their cages. Because they are tree-dwellers and never descend to the ground, they will need a number of tree branches or pieces of bark for climbing. If a wide, flat piece of bark is leaned against the side of the tank, they will usually select this sheltered spot to construct their webbed retreat.

Any kind of wood or bark (with the exception of resinous or oily woods like pine or cedar, which are toxic to your pet) will do. Most pet shops sell interestingly-shaped pieces of driftwood and cork bark for use in spider cages.

> **KEEPING CAGES CLEAN IS EASY**
>
> A properly maintained cage should be virtually odor-free, and because tarantulas are not messy animals, their cages do not need to be cleaned often. As long as you immediately remove all of the dead prey animals and the remains of meals, your spider cage will remain clean and trouble-free for years at a time. If you do not remove these wastes immediately, you are inviting a mite infestation.
>
> If you are keeping aggressive spiders, you will find both a long pair of tongs or forceps and a long spoon helpful for tasks such as removing dead prey animals, adding substrate or moving various bits of cage furniture around. Usually the tarantula will retreat to the bottom of its burrow while you are occupied with such tasks, but it is better to keep your fingers clear anyway.

Cork has the additional advantage of resisting infestation by mites. Pieces of bark from outside should be avoided, as they may contain mites or other parasites.

DECORATIONS

Many spider keepers like to place decorations inside the tank to give it a natural appearance. These are not needed by the tarantula, but they do no harm if properly planned. Rocks or other decorations should be securely anchored so that they do not fall or roll over and injure your spider. Live plants can be used in most spider tanks, where they provide humidity as well as an attractive appearance. Plastic plants are probably best, though, as they require no care and always look good. The widespread temptation to place live cactus plants in the tanks of desert tarantulas should be resisted, as the sharp spines present a potential danger to the spider.

Feeding
Your
Tarantula

Tarantulas, like all spiders, are carnivorous predators. They feed exclusively on small animals that they overpower and subdue with their venom apparatus. While it may be disturbing to some people, these spiders will usually eat only live food, and their feeding process is neither dainty nor delicate.

The good news is that feeding a captive tarantula is not a very difficult process. Unlike some exotic pets, spiders are usually good eaters, and even wild-caught tarantulas will eat willingly and with gusto. Most spiders are not particularly fussy in their choice of prey and will simply accept whatever suitably-sized food provided to them. Because their metabolism does not require a large energy input, tarantulas can get by on surprisingly small amounts of food, and a good meal every week is sufficient for most adult spiders (spiderlings, however, are growing furiously and need a much higher level of food intake).

Live Prey

Most experienced spider keepers recommend feeding your tarantula appropriately-sized live prey.

Appropriately-sized food animals are about one-half the size of the spider's body. In the case of prey animals that are defenseless and cannot cause any harm to the spider (such as earthworms), the food animal can be larger.

PURCHASING PREY ANIMALS

Most suitable prey animals can be found at any pet store that sells tarantulas or exotic pets. If you have a large number of spiderlings, however, or an extensive collection of adults to feed, it may be worth your while to begin raising food animals yourself.

Crickets are the most widely used food animals for raising tarantulas.

This ensures a steady supply of prey at various stages of size and development. None of these food sources is difficult to raise.

FRUIT FLIES

Fruit flies are an excellent staple food for hatchling tarantulas and very small spiderlings. They are used heavily in the study of genetics and are widely available from biological supply companies. In addition, tarantula breeders and dealers sometimes sell them. A colony of fruit flies is not difficult to maintain and takes up very little space.

There are two varieties of fruit fly that are best for feeding tarantulas. The vestigial winged flies have short, stunted wings and cannot fly. This presents several advantages; the flies cannot easily escape, and because they must walk around on the substrate, it is easier for the young spiderlings to find and capture them. There is also a variety of fruit fly that usually has no wings at all, but is capable of producing functional wings if the temperature rises too high.

Raising Fruit Flies

Fruit flies can be raised with a bare minimum of equipment. Any sort of bottle or jar can serve as a container (small plastic fruit juice jars are fine). It is best to sterilize the bottles using boiling water, in order to remove any mold or fungus spores that may infest your fly culture. Fly cultures should be kept in places that are warm and have subdued lighting. The flies breed best at temperatures of around 78°F.

Lids

The jars must have lids, both to keep the flies in and to prevent wild fruit flies from entering (if wild flies are allowed to mate with the vestigial-winged flies, the resulting generations will all have functional wings). The best lid is made from a plug of cotton wool or plastic foam inserted snugly into the top. This arrangement allows air to circulate but prevents the flies from moving in or out. Jars can also be sealed with a paper towel held tightly in place by rubber bands.

Feeding the Flies

The flies should be fed a mixture based on commercial dried potato flakes. Mix equal parts of potato flakes

FEEDING DURING DIFFERENT STAGES IN THE LIFE CYCLE

The species of prey animals suitable for feeding to a tarantula will change as the spider goes through its life cycle. Hatchlings and small spiderlings require very tiny prey, such as fruit flies and very young crickets. Older spiderlings can be offered somewhat larger prey, with mealworms being the usual choice. Subadult and adult spiders can be safely fed large crickets, and the truly giant spiders, such as the Goliath bird-eater or the king baboon, can be offered small vertebrate prey such as week-old mice.

Other appropriately-sized animals should also be offered from time to time for variety. These can include earthworms, beetles, grasshoppers, houseflies and moths. These prey animals can be captured outside and fed to your spider, provided that they have not been obtained in an area that was exposed to sprays or pesticides.

and water to form a paste, and sprinkle some baker's yeast on top. The paste should be about 1 inch deep at the bottom of the culture jar and should be thick enough so that it doesn't run when the jar is placed on its side. Some keepers place a small bit of plastic netting (the plastic canvas sold in sewing or craft shops works well for this) upright into the food paste, to give the flies and larvae something to climb on to get out of the gooey bottom; others omit the screen and allow the flies to simply walk up the sides of the jar.

Breeding

Place between ten and twelve flies in the jar and plug it up. The adult flies will mate and lay eggs on the damp food medium. Each adult female can lay around 500 eggs in a week. These hatch in a few days and produce tiny wormlike larvae, which will tunnel around in the food medium as they grow. After about a week, the larvae will crawl out of the medium and pupate, emerging as adult flies a few days later. The entire process takes about two weeks.

This vial, used here to house spiderlings, is usually used to breed fruit flies.

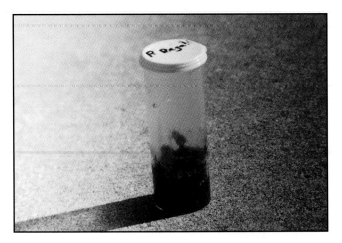

As the adult flies emerge, count out about a dozen of them and start a new culture. The rest of the adults are spider food. To remove them, simply upend the bottle and tap it until the flies fall out. A single culture bottle will produce flies for about six weeks, until the food medium becomes used up. By maintaining three or four cultures at a time and staggering them about a week apart, a continuous supply of adults is assured.

Lack of Nutrients in the Fruit Fly

There is a problem with using fruit flies as food for young tarantulas, however. Fruit flies are deficient in certain essential nutrients, and tarantulas that are fed an exclusive diet of fruit flies will develop abnormally. For this reason, about half of the spiderling's diet should consist of very young crickets or pinheads. This can also be supplemented with tiny wild-caught insects, such as aphids.

MEALWORMS

Mealworms are not actually worms at all, but are the immature larvae of the beetle species *Tenebrio molitor*. The adult insect is a black or dark brown beetle about 1 inch long. The larvae or mealworms look something like large fly maggots, up to 1 inch or so in length. They are a light straw color with darker heads.

Mealworms are a common prey animal for numerous insectivorous animals and are usually stocked by pet stores that sell fish, reptiles and spiders. Feeder mealworms are usually kept refrigerated so that they won't develop into adults. They are usually sold in small tubs containing 50 or 100 mealworms.

Raising Mealworms

To raise these animals you will need a starter colony of about fifty worms. A plastic sweater box makes a good container for raising beetles. Prepare a mixture of wheat bran,

---

REFUSAL TO EAT

In general, tarantulas should be given as much food as they will eat. Don't worry about overfeeding your spider—it will simply refuse to eat if it is not hungry. Periods of fasting are normal during the wintertime in many of the spiders from North America, and most tarantulas will also refuse food for a period of time before they shed their skin.

If your spider decides that it has had enough food for a while, make sure there are no live prey animals inside the cage with it. Prey animals like crickets are themselves carnivorous and can present a danger to the spider during periods of inactivity (especially during molting periods). Crickets will fight for their lives, and can present a serious hazard to very small tarantulas—they have strong jaws and may be able to penetrate the spider's exoskeleton and cause serious injury or death. Prey animals should be presented one at a time, and no additional food should be offered until the old food is gone. Crowded cages with too much decoration can make feeding difficult because they provide the prey animal with a variety of hiding spots and reduce the chances that it will walk into the spider's range.

instant oatmeal and powdered skim milk and fill the sweater box with about 2 inches of this medium. Cover the whole thing with a layer of slightly-damp paper towel, and add a few pieces of fresh fruit or lettuce for moisture. Add the mealworms and place the container in a warm (between 76° and 78°F), dark place. Replace the paper towel layer as it disintegrates.

The worms will tunnel through the cereal mixture, eating it as they go. After a few weeks, they will pupate and emerge as adult beetles. By always keeping about twenty adult beetles in the cage, a constant supply of new eggs can be assured. At room temperature, it takes about three months for the beetle to grow from an egg to an adult.

Be sure to remove any remains after the tarantula's meal.

Remove Uneaten Prey

There is a potential danger with mealworms that should be kept in mind— if the spider does not eat the mealworm, the worm may burrow into the substrate and live there where it can attack the tarantula after it molts. Make sure that any uneaten prey is removed immediately.

CRICKETS

Crickets are probably the most widely used food animals for raising tarantulas. Although crickets are widely available from pet and bait shops, finding a source of very small pinhead crickets can be a real problem for spiderling keepers. Therefore, if you have a lot of little hairy mouths to feed, it is probably best for you to raise your own food insects to ensure a steady supply.

Raising Crickets

Crickets breed readily in captivity, provided that they are given suitable conditions. Any large container with vertical space, such as an aquarium or a tall plastic sweater box, is suitable for raising crickets. The container should be lined with 2 inches of smooth tape (such as packing tape) along the top, just below the rim, to prevent the crickets from climbing out. Even with this precaution, though, a tight-fitting lid is still a necessity, and it should be well ventilated.

Feeding and Watering the Crickets

Place a number of cardboard egg containers or toilet paper rolls inside of the box. The crickets will use these for hiding and climbing. No substrate is necessary. Place the box in a warm, dark place where temperatures range between 85° and 90°F. At one end of the container, place a shallow bowl with water for drinking. Because crickets drown very easily, the water dish needs to be filled with gravel (or a sponge must be placed inside the dish) to allow them to climb out. The food dish should be next to the water.

Crickets require a high-protein diet. A good staple is dry dog or cat food, with a small amount of powdered skim milk sprinkled over it. This should be supplemented with pieces of potato, fresh fruit and leafy green vegetables. If they are not well-fed, the crickets will devour the cardboard—and each other. Every so often, you will need to break apart the breeding container, clean all of the dead crickets and feces out and replace all of the egg cartons or toilet paper rolls.

Breeding Crickets

An initial breeding stock of 500 adults can be obtained from a pet store or a cricket supplier. Because adult crickets live for less than two weeks, do not order your breeding stock until everything is set up and ready for them.

At the opposite end of the tank from the food and water, the crickets will need a substrate suitable for egglaying. Female crickets can be recognized by their long, straight ovipositor sticking out from the rear of their abdomen. This organ is used to deposit the eggs into damp soil or sand. A workable egglaying spot can be provided by filling a dish about 2 inches deep with a mixture of potting soil and sand. Cover this with a piece of ordinary window screening. This screen must be kept damp constantly. The females will poke their ovipositors between the screening and lay their eggs in the soil.

Every few days, the egglaying container should be removed and replaced with a fresh one. The old one should be placed in a smaller sweater box, equipped with water, food and hiding places in the same manner as the larger breeding container. It should be placed in a dark place with a temperature of around 90°F; at this temperature, the eggs will hatch in a few days to produce tiny crickets, known as pinheads. The pinheads are suitable for feeding to small spiderlings. As the young crickets grow, they can be fed to larger spiders. Once the young crickets have reached a length of ½ inch or so, about 100 of them should be transferred back to the breeding colony to replace the adults, most of which will have died by now. As the new youngsters mature, they also breed and begin the process anew. It is important to keep a constant supply of new adults introduced to the breeding colony because crickets have very short life spans.

Uneaten Crickets

Uneaten crickets in the cage can present a danger to the tarantula. If your spider does not eat a prey cricket within a few minutes, remove it so it does not establish itself or lay eggs in the substrate.

MICE

Only a few species of tarantula, including the king baboon, Goliath birdeater and the *Hysterocrates* species, will be able to handle prey as large as vertebrates. When used, they should not form the staple part of the diet and should be offered only as occasional treats. Keep in mind that adult mice have very sharp teeth that are capable of easily penetrating the exoskeleton of even the largest spider. Week-old mice that have not yet grown any fur are known as pinkies. They are defenseless, cannot bite and do not present any danger to the spider. Live pinkie mice are sometimes available from pet stores that cater to exotic animal keepers (they are also used to feed very young snakes). The tarantula owner must be aware that many mice are raised on a bedding of cedar or pine chips and, as mentioned before, these materials produce oils that are toxic to most arthropods. There is a remote possibility that some of the cedar oil will be clinging to the pinkie mouse's skin and be ingested by the tarantula. To avoid taking any chances, do not use any mice that have been exposed to cedar or pine.

Dead Food

Tarantulas prefer live prey, which they sense by touch. On some occasions, however, they can be deceived (temporarily) into eating dead food. One trick is to plaster a small ball of dog food or fresh meat onto the end of a piece of string and then dangle it just in front of the spider. Often, the tarantula will perceive the movement and seize the morsel as if it were live prey. However, the tarantula will get wise to this and may refuse to fall for it again.

FROZEN MICE

A few keepers have had some success in getting their spiders to eat prekilled, frozen and thawed pinkies or even adult mice. Although tarantulas usually hunt

This pinkie is about to become a meal.

by motion and vibration, they are also apparently capable of detecting the odor or taste of prey animals through the sensitive hairs on their legs and palps. Placing a dead mouse at the entrance of the burrow, where the tarantula will brush against it as it emerges in the night, may trigger a feeding response. If the spider does not eat the prekilled mouse after a short time, remove it before it begins to decompose.

Being a
Responsible

part three

Tarantula Owner

chapter 5

Handling
(or Not Handling)
Your Tarantula

Now we come to the part that everyone has the most questions about . . . to handle or not to handle.

The matter of handling tarantulas is extremely controversial among spider keepers. Some long-term tarantula keepers argue that they have developed a "way" with their animal (perhaps they have raised it from a tiny spiderling and are able to safely handle certain species that are normally considered aggressive). Other equally-experienced keepers argue that no tarantula should ever be handled. I suspect that the "best" answer lies somewhere between these extremes. Some species of tarantula are nasty and aggressive and will bite at the slightest provocation, and these should not be handled. On the other hand, part of the appeal of tarantula keeping as a hobby is the opportunity to handle and examine some of the more docile species at close range. There are no hard-and-fast rules—there will always be those who will not ever handle any of their spiders, and there will always be those who will attempt to handle some potentially unpleasant species.

Though you can be informed with the pros and cons, ultimately you are the only one who can decide whether the potential risks in handling your tarantula outweigh the benefits.

Safety Issues

Tarantulas are not "dangerous creatures" that crawl around looking for people to bite. In reality, they are basically shy and nonaggressive animals that are very content to sit placidly in their burrows watching the world go by and that will not bite unless they feel provoked or threatened. Nevertheless, there are some safety issues to be concerned with if you are going to keep tarantulas—particularly with some of the larger and more exotic species.

Always keep in mind that you are dealing with a venomous animal. Though there are no confirmed instances of anyone ever having died as a direct result of being envenomed by a tarantula, many species of tarantula are found in remote areas with virtually no medical facilities nearby (and thus virtually no medical records). In addition, the venom of many species has not been studied extensively. So, it is entirely possible that some species may have venom that can be dangerous to humans.

Potent Venom

At least two genera of tarantula are known to possess venom strong enough to produce more than a localized reaction. These are the genera *Pterinochilus* and *Poecilotheria*. Several members of these groups, including the Indian ornamental and varieties of Mosamba and Usumbara, are widely available as pets. People who have been bitten by these spiders describe a variety of symptoms.

One person who was bitten by a young *Pterinochilus* species described the pain as "several simultaneous wasp stings." The pain lasted for four hours, and the bitten finger was swollen for twenty-four hours. This person experienced stiffness in the joints of the bitten hand for over a year afterward. Another person who was bitten by a *Pterinochilus* spider experienced numbness in one arm and on the face.

The Usumbara produces a strong venom.

The members of the *Poecilotheria* genus seem to have the most potent venom and the worst bite. One person bitten by a young *P. regalis* experienced cramps, dizziness and difficulty breathing. He was kept in the hospital overnight for observation. Another person, bitten by the closely related *P. fasciata*, was put in the intensive care unit, suffering cramps, swelling and dizziness. A year later he still had recurring symptoms.

Other genera are sometimes reported to have produced systemic effects from a bite. People who have been bitten by Goliath birdeaters (*Theraphosa blondi*) have experienced nausea and cramps. One person bitten by a hercules tarantula (*Hysterocrates hercules*) reported numbness in the face, a feeling of coldness in the arms and cramping of the leg muscles. Togo starburst (*Heteroscodra maculata*) bites are also reported to have produced systemic symptoms, as are bites from spiders of the genera *Stromatopelma* and *Pseudotheraphosa*.

All of these symptoms indicate the presence of strong neurotoxins. Any spider from any of these genera should be suspected of having a virulent venom and should be treated with respect. They should not be handled.

ALLERGIC REACTIONS

Apart from the possible toxicity of the venom, there is an additional danger to which some people are vulnerable. Some people exhibit reactions to tarantula venom.

The signs of a mild allergic reaction to tarantula venom include a rash or hives, accompanied by itching and burning sensations. In stronger reactions, nausea, vomiting, cramps and diarrhea can appear. Any spider, no matter how weak the venom may be, is capable of producing an allergic reaction. Mild allergic reactions can be treated with antihistamines, and usually persist for only brief periods.

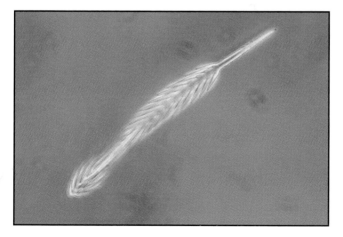

This is a magnified view of urticating hairs.

In a small percentage of people, however, the allergic reaction to tarantula venom may become so severe that it produces anaphylactic shock. For these people, the bite of a tarantula, no matter how weak the venom, is a life-threatening emergency that must be immediately addressed.

Victims of anaphylactic shock will experience tightening of the chest and difficulty breathing as the airway rapidly swells shut. Death can result in a matter of hours. The condition can be treated at the hospital emergency room with epinephrine.

FANGS AND URTICATING HAIRS

In any large tarantula, the mechanical effects of the bite should also be kept in mind. The fangs of a large

tarantula are massive—much larger in size than the fangs of some venomous snakes. They can produce painful wounds that are susceptible to infection.

Another potential problem can come from the urticating hairs found on most tarantula species from North or South America (the African

Never curl your fingers over your spider, this action will inevitably be perceived as threatening.

and Asian species are not known to have urticating hairs). These protective devices depend on mechanical action rather than venom or chemicals, but they can be extremely irritating and can produce an itchy rash that may last as long as two weeks.

In some species, most notably the *Theraphosa blondi*, the urticating affect can be severe. Tarantulas of the closely-related *Pseudotheraphosa* genus are even more dangerous, with urticating hairs that can travel through the air for considerable distances. Urticating hairs that get into the eyes or are inhaled into the throat can produce serious injury.

If you are doused with urticating hairs, rinse the affected area with water immediately to remove as many of the barbs as you can. Antihistamine creams, such as

Benadryl, can provide a bit of relief from the burning and itching. Some spider keepers use nonprescription H_2 blockers, such as Zantac, to ease the symptoms. Severe reactions may require a doctor to prescribe steroids as an anti-inflammatory measure. A number of people can also experience an allergic reaction to the presence of urticating hairs, which produces further symptoms independent of the urticating action itself.

Dangers to the Spider

In addition to all of these possible dangers to the handler, however, free-handling tarantulas can also be dangerous, even fatal, to the spider. The abdomen of a tarantula is very delicate, particularly in the ground-dwelling species, and any impact, such as a fall, can rupture the body wall and cause lethal injury. Falls of as little as 6 inches have killed captive spiders. The arboreal species are more accustomed to being up in the air and can leap to the ground from a considerable height—but only if they are prepared for it and the jump is voluntary.

Unlike cats, tarantulas cannot turn themselves in mid-air and land on their feet during an accidental fall. The spider may become startled by something and quickly leap or run off its keeper's hands, resulting in a fatal plunge to the floor. If the spider is handled roughly, it may be provoked to give a threat display or actually attempt to bite, which usually leads to the panic-stricken handler instinctively shaking the spider off.

Keep in mind, then, that any time a spider has its legs off the ground, it is at risk of fatal injury. If you plan to free-handle a docile spider, such as a redknee or pinktoe, it must be done carefully and correctly to avoid any mishaps. The overriding rule in handling spiders is this: If you feel nervous or anxious about holding a tarantula, then don't do it. Anxiety can lead to panic if a spider makes a sudden leap that will lead either to a fatal fall for the tarantula, or to you making an instinctive motion that the spider finds threatening, possibly leading to a bite (which is usually quickly followed by a fatal fall).

THE SPIDER'S VIEW

Spiders do not need to be free-handled (they probably find the whole experience to be extremely stressful), and many keepers go their whole lives without ever once touching their tarantulas. If you are not comfortable handling your spider, there is absolutely no reason why you must.

Safety Measures

GLOVES

A few handlers prefer to wear thick gloves when holding their spiders. This should be avoided, however, as it leads to clumsy and heavy-handed motions, which can frighten or injure the animal. Because the fangs of a tarantula can penetrate all but the thickest leather anyway, the "safety" provided by gloves is more psychological than actual. If you do not feel comfortable holding your spider without gloves, then it is probably best that you do not hold it at all.

DO NOT ANTAGONIZE YOUR SPIDER

A large percentage of bites result from the well-intentioned but reckless actions of keepers who wish to see their Usumbara or other pugnacious spider "do something" and who thus poke at it and prod it, or who attempt to extract an aggressive species from its burrow or shelter so that they can look at it. You will simply have to resign yourself to the facts: Tarantulas are not the most active animals and spend most of their time sitting there doing nothing; and, these spiders seldom emerge from their shelters except in the night and will not be often available for viewing.

> **DO NOT DISTURB!**
>
> Even docile species of tarantula can become defensive if they are disturbed inside their retreat. Never attempt to extract a spider from its shelter unless you need to, either to examine the spider and treat it for a medical condition, or to move it to another cage. Spiders that are intended to be handled often, for use in talks and shows for instance, should be maintained in a plain cage without a burrow (see chapter 3).

PROTECTING YOUR SPIDER

A few safety rules must be followed to protect your spider if you do choose to handle it. Spiderlings are too small and delicate to tolerate handling and should be left alone. As a fall will be fatal to most tarantulas, adult spiders should be held over the floor, no more than 6 inches above the surface. You should never hold a spider in your hands while you are standing up. Make sure there are no escape routes in the room because it is not unusual for an active spider to get away from you and make a run for it (they usually attempt to run up the walls to escape). Finally, do not handle your spider for at least two weeks before or after it sheds or molts.

A quiet retreat in the wild—tarantulas do not like to be disturbed.

Testing Your Spider

You should test the spider's reaction before attempting to actually pick it up. Using a pencil or artist's paintbrush, give the spider a gentle nudge at the back of the abdomen or one of the rear legs. A docile spider will react by raising the abdomen slightly or perhaps by taking a step or two away. Nervous or aggressive spiders will either run away or turn and rear up, baring their fangs. Species that possess urticating hairs may reach up with the back legs and brush off hairs toward the disturbance. Any of these are the arachnid equivalent to a snarling dog and mean that the spider doesn't want to be disturbed. Keep in mind that many of the African species will show no reaction at all to several pokes or prods (they are apparently hoping that the "threat" will not notice them and go away) before turning suddenly and attacking.

Some spiders will give fair warning first by sharply tapping the threat with the palps or front legs; others will simply bite without warning. You should only attempt to free-handle a spider that does not give a defensive reaction to being gently prodded with a pencil.

Test your spider to see if it is aggressive.

Picking Up Your Spider
Method #1

The simplest way to pick up and hold your spider is to place your hand flat in front of the tarantula and then gently tap it on the abdomen or rear legs with a finger or pencil. The spider will walk onto your outstretched palm. If the tarantula reaches up with its back legs and kicks urticating hairs from the top of its abdomen or if it turns around and rears up the front half of its body, it does not want to be disturbed and should not be handled.

Method #2

Another method of picking up a spider is riskier but can be used on particularly docile individuals. Place your index finger on top of the carapace, and then gently use your thumb and middle finger to grasp the spider by the cephalothorax, between the second and third pairs of legs, and lift it straight up. The spider may interpret this as an attack by a predator and may struggle initially, but once all of the legs leave the ground, it will be still. The spider can then be placed on the open palm of the other hand and released. This method of holding a spider is also useful if you need to examine its underside (for signs of mites or injury).

SCARED SPIDERS

More active spiders, especially arboreal species such as *Avicularia,* may be a bit more jumpy, and, if startled, may even attempt to run up your arm (you will feel it gripping your skin as it runs). If this happens, do not panic and attempt to shake the spider off, or you will almost certainly kill it. The tarantula will not usually attempt to bite as long as you stay still—it is merely carrying out its natural response to being frightened, which is to run higher up a tree. The spider will usually run to the top of your shoulder and stop there (it may also climb up your face or head, an experience that you will certainly never forget once it happens). Once the spider calms down and stops, it can be picked up again. If it gets into a spot that you cannot see or reach, you will need a friend to gently prod it onto an outstretched palm to get it off of you.

A scared spider may try to crawl up your arm, and may even wind up on top of your head!

Keep in mind, though, that the tarantula knows you are a living thing and a potential threat, and it is entirely capable of biting at any moment without warning.

Best Species for Handling

The only spiders that can be confidently handled regularly are the redknees and pinktoes. Most of the

North American members of the *Aphonopelma* genus are also pretty tolerant of being handled. There are some people who have experimented with handling such potentially nasty species as Goliath birdeaters and Trinidad chevrons. For the most part, however, particularly for beginners, handling any tarantula presents an unnecessary risk to both handler and spider and should be avoided unless it is absolutely essential to the well-being of the spider.

The redknee is one of the more docile breeds and is therefore one of the easiest to handle.

Handling Aggressive Spiders

It is, of course, sometimes necessary to remove an aggressive species of tarantula from its cage for cleaning or for treatment of medical problems. This should be done with great care—some of the more hostile spiders can move very quickly, and many can even run easily up the sides of a glass tank. Don't let the usually sedentary habits of these animals fool you; they are much faster than you are, and can easily escape or have their fangs embedded in your fingers before you even have time to react.

MOVING A NERVOUS OR RESISTANT TARANTULA

The best tool for moving nervous or belligerent spiders is an artist's soft-bristled paintbrush, about 1 foot long, with bristles about 1 inch wide. If you gently brush the spider's body or legs in the direction you want it to go, it will walk (or more probably run) in that direction.

If the tarantula is extremely aggressive, it may turn and bite the brush. If it does, you can usually slide it gently into a container while it hangs on with its fangs. Tarantulas can also be induced to move by gently blowing on them in the direction you want them to go. Most species of tarantula, particularly the burrowers, dislike being out in the open and when driven from one hiding place or burrow, tend to immediately dash into the nearest alternative shelter that they can find.

If you place a container in the spider's intended path, it will usually run right in and huddle inside. Snap the lid in place and your spider will be safely confined.

Another method of confining the spider so that it can be safely moved is to place a container upside down directly over the top of it; then, slide a piece of stiff cardboard underneath. The tarantula will walk up onto the cardboard or the sides of the container and can then be lifted out, container and all.

Releasing a Spider
CONTAINERS

To release a spider that has been confined in either of these manners, place the container in the cage and remove the lid carefully. If you unceremoniously dump the spider out, it may try to run up the sides of the tank. It is better to leave the whole thing in the cage until the tarantula decides to leave on its own. The empty container can then be lifted out later.

Handle with care! Irresponsible handling is dangerous—for the spider, for you and for the hobby.

IRRESPONSIBLE HANDLING

No tarantula should ever be taken out in public, except at planned preannounced shows or talks. And, under no circumstances should any arachnid be used in any sort of showing off or in an attempt to scare someone. Not only do such actions endanger the life of your spider, but they often serve as excuses for local or state governments (most of which already fear and misunderstand tarantulas) to pass laws restricting ownership of spiders and other "exotic animals."

Because of their inefficient respiratory and circulatory systems, however, tarantulas cannot run very far before they must stop for a rest. Once your spider stops to catch its breath, you can recapture it by carefully sliding a container over the top of it.

FISHNETS

A large aquarium fishnet also comes in handy for capturing escaped spiders. Be sure to use a net that is at least twice as large as the spider, or you may trap one of the tarantula's legs under the rim of the net and injure it.

WHAT NOT TO DO

Tarantulas should *never* be grasped by the abdomen, as too much pressure will rupture it and kill the spider. Also, keep in mind that the legs tear off very easily and can produce serious bleeding. Be careful that you do not pin or pull on any of the spider's appendages while you are holding it. Finally, do not ever close your fist around a spider or curl your fingers over the top of it while you are holding it—it will certainly view this as an attack and will respond defensively.

Docile species such as redknees will walk slowly from palm to palm, stopping often for rests. Be very careful that you do not breathe heavily on the spider, as this will startle it. Even the slowest species are capable of a quick burst of speed, and a spider that is frightened can make a sudden leap, which can lead to a fall. Also, keep in mind that tarantulas have claws in their feet, which may become entangled in clothing, particularly loosely-woven fabric like sweaters.

ADDITIONAL TRANSFER PRECAUTIONS

One safety precaution you can take when transferring a fast species (particularly spiderlings) to a new cage is to place both the old and new homes into a large plastic box and line the top 4 inches or so of this container with petroleum jelly. If the spider gets away from you and attempts to escape, it will not be able to pass this barrier and can be recaptured relatively easily and maneuvered into its new home.

If you carry out the transfer operation in an empty bathtub (make sure the drain is plugged), it will be more difficult for the spider to get away from you.

If you place the entire spider cage in the refrigerator for about fifteen minutes before attempting to remove the spider, its metabolism will be slowed down and it will not be able to run as quickly. Be very careful that you do not chill the spider too long or it will die (it should not be cooled to the point where it can no longer move around). The idea here is to slow the spider down, not to immobilize it completely. Note that this method should not be used with tropical species.

6

Caring
for Your
Tarantula

For the most part, tarantulas are hardy animals that are not prone to disease or sickness. This is fortunate, as you are not likely to ever find a veterinarian anywhere who will know very much about your spider's physiology or care. Most likely, when it comes to protecting the health of your pet, you will be completely on your own.

Happily, the list of potential spider ailments is rather short. The following is a list of the most common health problems faced by captive spiders, along with some suggested courses of action to deal with them.

Anorexia

Anorexia is the general term for refusal to eat. It is almost always the result of some sort of environmental problem. If your spider refuses food for more than three or four weeks and is not showing any signs of an impending molt (such as a dark patch under the bald spot on the abdomen, or spinning a mat to lie on during shedding), there may be a condition that needs to be corrected.

The first thing to check is the temperature. Because spiders are ectotherms, they are dependent upon outside sources of heat to maintain their body temperatures. If their cage is too cool they will not be able to maintain their activities and will stop eating. Most tarantulas stop eating if the temperature in their cage drops below 75°F or so.

Always watch the temperature of your spider's cage.

The next thing to check is the humidity level. Tarantulas (even the desert species) require a moderate level of humidity. If conditions are too dry for them, they will often hole up in their shelter or burrow (where the humidity level is locally higher), plug it up with silk and wait out the dry spell. A sufficient level of humidity in the tank will entice them to emerge and become active again.

Off-feed

Keep in mind that captive tarantulas often go "off-feed" for long periods of time for no apparent reason, only to begin eating again as if nothing had happened. Some captive spiders have refused food for over two years and emerged without any apparent health problems. If the temperature and humidity are in the proper range and your spider is still not eating, there is probably nothing wrong. Just keep offering some different food animals periodically, and your tarantula will eat again when it is hungry.

Mites

Mites are probably the most common problem faced by tarantula keepers. You may actually see the mites crawling on the substrate or on the spider. They will look like small, light-colored moving dots. If your spider is standing on tiptoe with its legs stretched and its body high off the ground, it is a pretty good sign that the cage is infested with mites (the spider is trying to get as far away from the infested substrate as it can).

Mites are attracted to potential food sources, and in a tarantula's cage, this usually means discarded food carcasses and wastes. The best way to avoid a mite problem, therefore, is to keep the tarantula's cage scrupulously clean and to remove any prey remains as soon as possible.

TREATMENTS
Stop Misting the Cage

Removing a mite infestation once it occurs can be quite a task. Because using any sort of insecticide is not an option (it would kill your spider as well as the invaders), other methods must be used. Several methods take advantage of the fact that mites are very small—their entire body is smaller in diameter than your spider's cuticle. Because of this, they have a high surface-to-volume ratio and lose moisture much more quickly than your spider. One way to get rid of mites, then, is to make the conditions so dry that they desiccate and die.

This can be done in several ways. One simple solution is to temporarily stop misting the tarantula's cage and allow it to dry out for a short period of time. The tarantula must be provided with a drinking dish during this time to prevent it from becoming dehydrated along with the mites.

Powdering

Another trick, which works well if the infestation is not too heavy, is to brush some talcum powder onto the spider's body. The powder acts as a sponge and absorbs moisture, drying out and killing any mites that come in contact with it. Again, the spider must be given access to drinking water during this time. These methods cannot be used with certain species, such as *H. gigas* or *T. blondi*, which need high humidity levels to survive.

Regular Cleanings

If the mite infestation is heavy, the best solution is to clean out the entire cage, replacing all of the substrate and furniture. The cage itself should be wiped down with a weak bleach solution—use one capful of bleach to one bucketful of water and rinse the cage thoroughly with plain water afterwards. You will also have to treat any shelving, flooring and any other surfaces that the cage has been near, as mites will often wander far afield to lay their eggs, and even a small number of surviving eggs can begin a new population explosion.

Even after this treatment, however, a number of pests will still be present, hiding on the spider itself. These can sometimes be removed by carefully picking them off the tarantula's body with a cotton swab that has been dipped in petroleum jelly or olive oil, but it is still unlikely that you will get them all. Each night, the mites will leave the spider's body temporarily to breed and lay eggs in the substrate. In the morning, then, if you replace all of the substrate, you will be removing a good portion of the remaining mites as well as all of the eggs they have laid. By systematically cleaning the cage every day for a week or two, you may be able to reduce the mite's population level to the point where it remains under control and isn't a problem. The mite population may even die out completely.

Predatory Mites

Some tarantula keepers prefer to use a form of biological warfare to combat a mite infestation. A number of tarantula dealers sell stocks of the predatory mite species *Hypoaspis miles*. These tiny predators feed on other species of mites, including those that infest your spider's cage. Although they are harmless to the tarantula, they will scour it completely, killing and eating every mite they come across. Once the "bad" mites are gone, the predatory *Hypoaspis* will begin feeding on each other, eventually reducing their own population

*Knowing how to
heal your taran-
tula will ensure
that it remains
healthy.*

to the point where they cannot reproduce anymore
and will all starve, thus removing themselves from the
tank.

Cuts and Wounds

Even an extremely minor wound or cut can be life-
threatening to a spider. The most common cause of
tears and wounds is improper handling—usually
occurring when a tarantula is dropped or falls from a
height.

LEGS

Sometimes legs will become trapped under cage lids
and break or tear open. Tears on the leg will usually
be dealt with by the spider itself, tearing off the old leg
at the cephalothorax (as mentioned previously, this is
called autotomy). Special muscles in the body close off
the remaining stump to halt the bleeding.

REMOVING AN APPENDAGE

If your spider has an injured leg and hasn't auto-
tomized by itself, it may be necessary for you to remove
the injured appendage. Using a pair of tweezers or for-
ceps, tear into the leg by the base and pull it sharply
upwards. This will induce the spider to voluntarily cast
off the leg, breaking it at the joint between the coxa
and trochanter. The lost leg will be regenerated and
replaced over the next few molts.

A leak or tear in the body wall is a more serious matter and can require some drastic measures on your part. A bleeding spider will exude a clear or pale blue liquid. This is life-threatening and must be dealt with immediately.

Treating a wounded spider requires you to have intimate contact with it. If you have an aggressive or potentially dangerous spider, you will need to render it incapable of resisting, using one of the methods described in chapter 5, or by anesthetizing it, as discussed later in this chapter.

PATCHING SMALL TEARS

Small tears can usually be patched without too much trouble. Such wounds can usually be sealed with a dab of petroleum jelly or by drugstore preparations used by humans. Once the bleeding is stopped, the spider will be induced to begin a shed cycle, and the cuticle will be repaired at the next molt.

LARGE WOUNDS

Large, gaping wounds, such as those produced by a fall, require drastic and immediate measures. The best thing to do is seal the wound completely by using a tube of ordinary Super Glue (the thick gel-type is easiest to apply). Most of the components in glue are potentially toxic to your spider, and this remedy may kill it, but the spider is doomed to certain death without this type of treatment. After suffering any type of wound or cut, your tarantula will be severely dehydrated. Make sure it has access to drinking water for some time after it heals.

Fungus and Mold

Spider tanks that are kept too damp or that have insufficient ventilation often become infested with various types of molds and fungi, which appear as cottony tufts in the substrate. Sometimes spots of fungus will appear on the spider's skin. If not checked, these pests can invade the lining of the tarantula's booklungs and kill it.

The most effective way to treat a mold or fungus infestation is to remove the conditions that promote its growth. Increase the air flow in the cage and stop spraying for a few days to allow the substrate to dry out. This should kill the fungus. Make sure the spider has access to drinking water during this time.

Dehydration

Although many of the tarantulas commonly kept as pets are desert-dwellers and are adapted to hot, dry conditions, they do require a source of water and do maintain relatively humid conditions inside their burrows. Humidity is particularly important during molting time—if conditions are too dry during the molt, the new exoskeleton may either crack and bleed at the joints, or it may adhere to the old skin and be torn.

Dehydrated spiders can be recognized by their shriveled abdomens and their jerking and unsteady gait. Treatment is simple—place a shallow water dish in front of the spider and allow it to drink as much as it wants.

Molting

Many beginning tarantula keepers are shocked one morning when they look into their spider's cage only to find what looks like a second spider. Others may be dismayed to see their tarantula lying on its back with its feet in the air, apparently dead. Both are normal parts of the process of ecdysis, or molting the old cuticle and growing a new one.

The molting process is a normal occurrence for all arthropods. Young spiders shed as often as once a month. Subadults shed three or four times a year, and adults shed only once a year. Female tarantulas will molt throughout their lives; males stop molting once they reach sexual maturity.

The exoskeleton is rigid and cannot grow. So, as the spider gets larger it must be periodically shed. Molting is also usually brought on after an injury to or tear in the exoskeleton.

During molting, hormones cause a new layer of chitin to grow beneath the old one, separated by a thin layer of fluid. The spider will stop eating for a period of several weeks. To shed, the spider seeks out a sheltered spot, spins a thick mat of silk and lies on its back. (This applies only to terrestrial spiders. Arboreal tarantulas will molt inside their silken retreats.) At this point, some inexperienced spider keepers, supposing the spi der to be dead or dying, have reached in to place the tarantula right-side-up and have thereby unknowingly killed it. (Shedding tarantulas lie on their back with their legs extended in the air. Dead spiders are always lying on their belly with their legs tightly curled underneath.)

To shed, the tarantula splits the old exoskeleton open along the side of the carapace and carefully withdraws all of its legs from the old cuticle. The entire exterior of the spider is replaced, including all of the hair, all of the appendages (including the fangs) and even the delicate lining of the booklungs and genital opening. In young spiders, this process may take a matter of minutes. In adults, the molting process may take all night.

STUCK!

If the spider is completely stuck inside the old exoskeleton or if all or most of the legs are trapped and cannot be released, the tarantula is doomed. Place it in the freezer overnight to end its suffering, and consider the experience a hard-learned lesson on the importance of keeping a suitable humidity level in the tank.

Immediately after shedding, the new cuticle is soft and flexible. The tarantula will now flip back over onto its legs and stretch out widely, allowing the new exoskeleton to dry and harden. During this time, the spider is extremely vulnerable to tears and rips in the cuticle, which is susceptible to fatal bleeding. For this reason, do not touch or attempt to handle your tarantula for at least a week after it has shed its skin; the new cuticle needs time to dry and harden sufficiently. Also, make sure that no crickets or other prey animals are in the tank during the molting process, as tarantulas have been attacked, killed and eaten by crickets while they were helpless during the molt.

Tarantulas should not be fed until at least a week after a shed, and many times they will refuse food for a period of weeks until they feel safe again.

SHEDDING PROBLEMS

If the environmental conditions are too dry during the molt, the old exoskeleton may adhere to the new one, trapping the spider. If only one or two legs are stuck and cannot be withdrawn it may be possible to mist the old cuticle with water and gently work it off. If the old skin cannot be detached, it may be best to induce autotomy by pulling off the trapped legs. The spider will get along without them until its next molt.

This spider has a clearly visible bald spot.

HAIR LOSS

Some inexperienced keepers become alarmed to see large bald spots appearing on their tarantula's abdomen, believing this to be a sign of mange or some other disease. In reality, this is quite normal and is nothing to worry about. Most North and South American spiders have urticating hairs on the back of their abdomen, which they scrape off and fling at predators or other potential threats. These hairs are replaced during the molt, and your now-bald spider will look as good as new after the next shed.

Keep in mind, though, that constant shedding of urticating hairs means that the spider is being unduly stressed by something that it finds threatening. Either it is being handled too often or it is being frightened by movement outside its cage.

Parasitic Flies and Wasps

Wild tarantulas are preyed upon by a variety of parasitic insects. Some species of fly and wasp lay their eggs on the spider's exoskeleton. When the maggot hatches, it burrows into the spider's body cavity, where it feeds until it emerges to pupate, killing the spider.

The chances of such a parasite finding your spider are pretty remote (unless your spider is wild-caught and brought a parasite along with it). If you are so unfortunate as to have purchased a wild-caught spider with parasites, there is not really much you can do for it. Make sure you isolate the spider so that the emerging parasites do not infect any other members of your collection.

Life-threatening Situations

In some cases, it may be necessary to completely immobilize a tarantula. This is a risky procedure that can be fatal to the spider, so it should not be used except to deal with a life-threatening situation such as an injury to the exoskeleton. If an aggressive species receives such an injury, rendering the spider insensible and incapable of biting may be the only safe way for you to administer treatment and save its life.

CARBON DIOXIDE ANESTHETIC

The best method of "knocking out" a tarantula is to use carbon dioxide gas. The idea is to replace all of the oxygen in the spider's booklungs with carbon dioxide, which will cause it to become immobilized (if deprived of oxygen for too long, however, it causes the spider to collapse, lose consciousness and die).

Immobilization can be accomplished by placing the spider in a plastic container (one without air holes along the bottom). Place some baking soda in a small dish inside the tank and add some vinegar. The resulting chemical reaction produces carbon dioxide gas, which, since it is heavier than air, stays at the bottom of the tank—right where the spider is. As the gas enters its booklungs, the spider will run around frantically at first, then it will slow down, begin to stagger as if it were drunk and finally sit still. The whole process takes about fifteen to twenty minutes.

As soon as the spider has been slowed enough to handle, remove it from the gas. As soon as the tarantula has been removed from the carbon dioxide, oxygen will begin entering its system again, and it will begin to recover. It usually takes about the same length of time for the spider to regain its senses as it did for it to go under. This will give you about ten minutes to do what you need to do with it before it is able to resist.

Because this process is very risky and could kill your spider, it is worth repeating that this procedure should only be followed when absolutely necessary to save the life of a seriously injured and bleeding tarantula. The "refrigeration" method is much safer.

chapter 7

Tarantula
Conservation

When most people think of endangered species, they think of big and spectacular animals such as elephants, tigers or manatees. They usually do not think of spiders. Spiders and tarantulas, however, being part of the natural world, are affected by habitat loss and overcol-

lection just as are other living things. A number of tarantula species from around the world are being threatened with extinction and are now being given the same legal protections that are bestowed upon other threatened or endangered species.

Overharvesting

The current plight of the redknee illustrates what can happen to wild populations when the pet trade runs amok. In the 1970s, these spiders were taken from the Mexican deserts at a prodigious rate to feed the exotic pet market in the United States and Europe. Every local pet store was likely to have several of these spiders, available for as little as $10 each.

Unfortunately, there was no large-scale captive breeding of tarantulas being carried out, and nearly all of these individuals were taken directly from the wild. Rampant overharvesting soon led to a sharp drop in population levels, and *Brachypelma smithi* is now listed on international treaties as a threatened species—the only species of animal known to have been threatened with extinction predominantly because of the pet trade. It is now illegal to take this species from the wild for international trade without a permit.

Fortunately, since the 1970s our knowledge of captive spiders has increased enormously, and captive breeding is now almost a routine affair. These beautiful and hardy spiders are now once again available in the pet trade, usually as captive-bred spiderlings.

The Mexican red-knee has become a symbol of how irresponsible overharvesting practices can endanger animals in the wild.

International Treaties

The most important international effort to protect wildlife is the Convention on the International Trade in Endangered Species, known as CITES. Under CITES, protected animals are divided into two groups. Animals listed under CITES Appendix I are those that are in immediate danger of extinction. With the exception of zoos under special permit, it is illegal to import or export any of these animals.

Animals listed under CITES Appendix II are not yet in imminent danger of extinction, but are declining rapidly and must be given protection. It is illegal to import or export any of these species unless they were captured under a special permit or unless they were captive-bred.

The primary purpose of the CITES treaty is to prevent the international smuggling of endangered or threatened animals that have been taken from the wild Wildlife smuggling is a serious problem; according to some Interpol estimates, illegal wildlife trade is a $6 billion a year business, placing it just behind illegal drug trafficking and just ahead of illegal arms smuggling.

A number of tarantula species are currently protected under provisions of the CITES treaty, and several more will probably be CITES listed sometime in the next few years. The entire *Brachypelma* genus, found in Mexico and Central America, is listed under Appendix II of the CITES treaty. This genus includes such popular staples of the pet trade as the Mexican redknee, the redrump and the redleg. The Mexican redknee, *B. smithi*, was listed under CITES after the pet trade led to overcollection, which caused the wild population to dwindle to dangerously low levels. The other members of the *Brachypelma* genus are also popular in the pet trade, and are found only in isolated areas in the wild, leaving them potentially vulnerable to similar overcollection. Fortunately, most members of this genus breed rather easily in captivity, making them widely available to hobbyists and collectors without the necessity of taking any more individuals from the wild.

OTHER THREATENED SPECIES

After the redknee gained legal protection, it was largely replaced in the pet trade by the Chilean rose, *Phrixotrichus spatulata*. Recently, however, there have been some indications that the pet trade is beginning to reduce the numbers of this species in the wild, and because the rose tarantula is found only in a limited geographic area, near the Atacama Desert in Chile, the odds are pretty good that it will soon be CITES II listed as well.

Unfortunately, this species is rather difficult to breed in captivity and is not often found as captive-bred spiderlings. Unless research leads to an effective way of inducing these spiders to breed in captivity, they may become extremely rare once their export is banned by CITES, and they will more than likely completely disappear from the pet trade.

There is some evidence that the pet trade may now be depleting the supply of the Chilean rose from the wild.

The large *Theraphosa* species are natives of tropical rain forests in South America, and have been disappearing at alarming rates due to logging and agricultural clearing. The biodiversity of these tropical areas has only begun to be catalogued, and it is likely that many unknown species of tarantula will disappear forever—killed off by habitat loss before they have even been described by science. As a result of this habitat loss, many tropical spiders face a real possibility of extinction, and, although they are not yet CITES listed, such a step may become necessary within a few years. Several South American countries already regulate the export of their native tarantulas.

As large areas of India and southern Asia continue to be deforested by humans, the members of the *Poecilotheria* genus are similarly being threatened with habitat loss. Already, members of the American Tarantula Society have begun discussing methods of facilitating captive breeding of "pokes" to help ensure their survival and to reduce the need to take any more of them from the wild.

State Laws

In addition to international CITES regulations, some individual states within the U.S. have passed regulations intended to prevent the introduction of nonnative species. The most important of these to tarantula keepers is the state of Florida, which has outlawed the import of two tarantula genera, the *Avicularia* pinktoes and the *Phormictopus* genus, which includes the Haitian brown tarantula. Authorities have concluded that these two genera are adaptable enough to possibly become established in Florida (a state which already suffers from the inadvertent introduction of a large number of nonnative animal and plant species). To prevent this and to protect its own native wildlife, Florida has legally banned the ownership (and thus the release, intentionally or otherwise) of these species.

With the exception of these few laws designed to protect threatened species, the trading and keeping of tarantulas is largely unregulated in the United States. As the hobby of tarantula keeping continues to grow, however, this situation is very likely to change. Irresponsible owners who are either bitten by aggressive species or who stupidly show off or scare others with their spiders will provoke increasing numbers of local or state regulations limiting the ownership of spiders or, more likely, banning them outright.

While increasing legal regulation of tarantula keeping in the near future is probably inevitable, it is up to responsible spider keepers to ensure that laws are made in an atmosphere of informed discussion, rather than ignorant hysteria and fear. Others must be educated about these unique animals and the role they play in their ecosystems—to show others that tarantulas are shy and nonaggressive creatures, not the vicious killers that live only in the imaginations of B-movie writers. The future of tarantula keeping as a hobby may be at stake.

Captive Breeding

One of the most concrete contributions that tarantula hobbyists can make towards conservation is a vigorous and steady program of captive breeding. One of the chief threats facing many wild populations of tarantulas, both within the United States and abroad, is over-collection for the pet trade. As the popularity of spider keeping continues to grow, pressure on wild populations will grow with it, bringing the distinct possibility that other species may suffer the same fate at the hands of collectors as the Mexican redknee did in the 1970s.

One solution to this problem is to encourage captive breeding of tarantula species, so they can be made available to hobbyists and collectors without the necessity of taking any more animals from the wild.

Captive breeding helps to keep the numbers of tarantulas in the wild constant.

Even if you do not plan to breed spiders yourself, if you find yourself with a fully mature male with mating hooks, you should give serious thought to sending it out on breeding loan. Any of the tarantula societies will be able to provide you with a list of hobbyists who have adult females of your species available for breeding. The usual arrangement is for the owner of each spider to split the resulting offspring fifty-fifty. If for whatever reason you do not want to keep any of the offspring, donate them to someone who will continue to breed them. While mating may present an element of risk to your spider (some female tarantulas will kill the male either before or after mating), your mature male is almost at the end of its life and hasn't very long to live in any case.

If you have a species rarely kept in captivity, it is particularly important for it to be bred before it dies. Of course many tarantula species, including some commonly kept species such as the Chilean rose and the king baboon, have proven to be difficult to breed in captivity. This usually means, however, that we simply do not yet know enough about their biology and habits to duplicate them in captivity. It therefore becomes a priority for serious hobbyists to identify the conditions under which these spiders can be kept and breeding induced. Such knowledge will be vital to protecting and maintaining these species—and serious amateurs are fully capable of discovering and providing such knowledge.

Educational Talks and Shows

Perhaps the single most important factor in protecting and preserving arachnids, as well as other animals, is public education. Few other groups of animals have been maligned for so long as have tarantulas. Most people have, at best, only a vague understanding of these animals, and most of what they do "understand" is negative and usually inaccurate. For this reason, it is important to exhibit and display spiders and other arachnids in appropriate locales, so people can be educated about the vital roles they play within various ecosystems.

If you are comfortable with public speaking, a large number of groups and organizations can serve as potential sites for an educational lecture or show about spiders. Contact the biology teachers in your local school districts, as well as scout troops, conservation clubs, local environmental organizations and any other group of people that may have an interest in unusual pets, the outdoors or ecology and wildlife. Many of these groups have guest lecturers at their meetings and would be happy to allow you to speak to their members.

There are two basic formats for any educational show. The first option is the static display, in which various animals are presented in cages, and the keeper sits or stands nearby and is available to answer questions. This format is the easiest to set up and involves the least amount of work on the part of the hobbyist. It may also be best for the person who isn't comfortable speaking formally in front of a group but who doesn't mind talking one-on-one.

Animals to be used in these educational displays must be selected carefully, keeping a number of criteria in mind. To be attractive to an audience, they should be both visually interesting and readily viewable. As a trip to the zoo will demonstrate, the displays that get the most audience attention are those that contain active animals out in the open; those which simply look like an empty tank are quickly passed by. Spiders that skulk in hiding places or bury themselves in substrate are not suitable for display, and species that are severely stressed by being exposed to view should also be avoided.

All animals (particularly those that are aggressive or potentially dangerous, such as birdeaters and baboons) should be securely caged in a manner that does not allow enterprising audience members to get their fingers in the cage. All animal cages should be securely locked, both to prevent possible escapes and to safeguard the animals from audience attempts to touch or pet them.

Because the attention span of many audiences (particularly of youngsters) is rather limited, the display should be as varied as possible. A good mix of different sizes and colors will keep the display interesting and attractive.

The other, more common format for an educational presentation is the active display, in which the audience is gathered together in a group, with the speaker standing in front of them holding and presenting individual animals. I prefer this approach because it allows me to directly communicate the

JOIN THE AMERICAN TARANTULA SOCIETY

Despite the widespread notoriety of tarantulas and the growing interest in keeping them in captivity, very little biological research has been carried out on these animals, and large gaps exist in our knowledge of their habits and behavior. To encourage and support further study of tarantulas and other arachnids, the American Tarantula Society (ATS) was formed, with members running the gamut from professional arachnologists to interested amateur hobbyists. (Similar organizations also exist in Britain and Holland.) ATS disseminates information on the captive care and breeding of tarantulas and other arachnids and also supports field research into tarantula biology, taxonomy and behavior.

Because so little professional research has been done, arachnology is one of the few remaining areas of science where interested amateurs can still make important discoveries on their own through careful observation. For many tarantula species, even such basic information as life span, clutch size and growth rate are entirely unknown. ATS, and its journal, *Forum*, allows dedicated amateur scientists to discover such information and make it available to others.

particular information I want to convey about any specific animal, and it avoids the problem of endlessly repeating answers to the same questions from different people.

Only the most docile tarantulas should be actively handled during these talks. The audience should be warned beforehand to not attempt to touch, poke, blow on or in any other way disturb the spiders. Red-knees (*B. smithi*) and pinktoes (*Avicularia* species) are usually calm and docile and do not spook very easily.

In all my talks, I prefer to arrange the audience into a semicircle or U-shape, while I have my animals at a table behind me (having the animals out of view allows the audience to focus their attention on me and the arachnid currently being displayed, rather than

Potentially harmful spiders, such as the king baboon, must be secured extremely well.

looking anxiously to see what's ahead). I display each animal one at a time, giving a short talk about some particular aspect of its biology or lifestyle as I slowly carry it around the semicircle to allow everyone to see it closely.

One of the best ways to gauge the interest of the audience is by how many questions they ask. If the audience is attentive and asks a lot of questions, you are doing a good job of communicating information to them. If, on the other hand, the audience is sitting stone-faced and silent, your talk is not going so well.

Because the audience will take what you say at face value, be sure that your information is accurate, and answer any questions put to you as concisely as you can. If you do not know the answer to a question, admit it and suggest places where the questioner can learn this information. At all times, you should appear relaxed and confident—lecturers who appear tense and nervous tend to make their audiences feel tense and nervous, too. The point of your talk is to reduce people's fear and anxiety about arachnids, not to add to it.

part four

Beyond the Basics

chapter 8

Resources

Tarantula Societies

American Tarantula Society
P.O. Box 1617
Artesia, NM 88211-1617

British Tarantula Society
81 Phillimore Place
Radlett
Hertfordshire WD7 8NJ
United Kingdom

Dutch Tarantula Society
Gert Baarda
Roderwolderdijk 10
9744 TG, Groningen
Holland

Recommended Reading

Unfortunately, there isn't much information available in print for the captive care of tarantulas. These are the books that are most helpful to beginners:

Baerg, W. J. *The Tarantula.* London UK: Fitzgerald Publishing, 1997.

Breene, Robert G. Ed. *Common Names of Arachnids.* Artesia, N.M.: American Tarantula Society, 1997.

Foelix, Rainer F. *Biology of Spiders.* New York: Oxford University Press, 1996.

Marshall, Sam. *Tarantulas and Other Arachnids.* Hauppauge, N.Y.: Barron's Educational series, 1996.

Schultz, Stanley and Marguerite Schultz. *The Tarantula Keeper's Guide.* Hauppauge, N.Y.: Barron's Educational Series, 1998.

Internet Resources

The Internet is a valuable resource for any tarantula keeper. Here are some of the sites you will find while surfing the Web:

Doug's Tarantula Page
http://www.concentric.net/~Dmartin

Dave's Tarantula Page
http://www.geocities.com/Yosemite/2448/Arachnid.html

Arachnophile Page
http://www.geocities.com/RainForest/5201

Popular Pet Tarantulas
http://inetc.net/Tarantulas

Tarantulas as Pets
http://concentric.net/~Lottery/spiders.shtml

Scorpion du Jour Page
http://wrbu.si.edu/stockwell/du_jour/scorpion_du_jour.html

Arachnid E-Mail List
http://www.realtime.net/~welbon/spiders.html

Scorpion Enthusiasts E-Mail List
http://wrbu.si.edu/stockwell/list/list.html

Readers can also feel free to e-mail me, at
lflank@rocketmail.com.

Tarantula Breeders and Dealers

Arachnocentric
P.O. Box 411147
Chicago, IL 60641

ATS Pet Shop
American Tarantula Society
P.O. Box 1617
Artesia, NM 88211-1617

Genie's Teenie Weenies
P.O. Box 161
Glace Bay, Nova Scotia
B1A 5V2
Canada

Glades Herp
P.O. Box 50911
Ft. Myers, FL 33905

Special Care Pet Center
5 West Prospect Ave.
Pittsburgh, PA 15205

Spiderpatch
10315 Avis Ln.
Santee, CA 92071-4432

West Coast Zoological
P.O. Box 720849
San Diego, CA 92172-0849

**Crickets, Fruit Flies, Mealworms
and Other Foods**
Carolina Biological Supply
2700 York Rd.
Burlington, NC 27215

Fluker Farms
1333 Plantation Ave.
Port Allen, LA 70767

Grubco
P.O. Box 15001
Hamilton, OH 45015

Reeves Cricket Ranch
31585 Rd. 68
Visalia, CA 93291

Top Hat Cricket Farm
1919 Forest Dr.
Kalamazoo, MI 49002

Rockingham Public Library
540-434-4475
Harrisonburg, Virginia 22801